THE
PELOPONNESE
CASTLES & MONASTERIES

EDITIONS
TOUBI'S ®
ΕΚΔΟΣΕΙΣ

Texts edited by: YORGOS VOYIATZIS
Photographs: Y. YANNELOS, Y. DESYPRIS, Y. KOUMOUROS,
P. SPYROPOULOS, Archive: M. TOUBIS

Art editing by: NORA ANASTASOGLOU
Photosetting, colour separation, montage, printed: GRAPHIC ART M. TOUBIS S.A.

mail toubis@compulink.gr

*The Olympic flame in ancient Olympia and its conveyance to the place where
the Olympic Games are being held an event established for the Olympiad of 1936.*

The Peloponnese! One of the most important regions in Greece where civilization rose to one of its greatest heights, where myth developed into legendary history and where unrivalled art has left its indelible traces, revealing human magnificence. The Peloponnese is a the land of ancient history, possessed of fascinating myths and living traditions as can be seen in its legendary acropolises, medieval castles, moribund Byzantine towns and its countless other historical monuments.

The Peloponnese was the cradle of the fabulous Mycenean civilization, the homeland of the stalwart men of Leonidas, the gallant Spartans. Here is Olympia, the source of the inextinguishable Olympic flame and the glorious athletic ideal that had the power to halt wars and unite enemies, for the duration of the Olympic Games.

Here is where the statue of Olympian Zeus was found, one of the Seven Wonders of the ancient world, one of the masterpieces of the famous sculptor Pheidias. Here is where one still finds the marvelous ancient theater at Epidaurus where so many distinguished performances have been produced, continuing right down to the present-day.

Here one still can find the Byzantine town of Mistra and the Mani as wild as ever. Nature has endowed the Peloponnese with exceptional beauty. Peaceful landscapes stand alongside ones of more savage beauty, the lofty summits of the mountains soar above the spreading plains, superb sand beaches line the leeward bays but there are also steep and imposing cliffs; all these alternate with one another in an endless dance. Green and blue are the dominant colors in most areas. The earth offers one the bounty of its fruitfulness. It area has abundant running water and its lakes, such as Stymphalia, lend the landscape a dreamlike aspect. Deep shady valleys and ravines snake down through the high mountain ranges and the caves call forth both awe and admiration. The towns, both small and large, each with its own special color and character, add the final touches to the composition: all the way from historic Nafplio to romantic Monemvasia and from mountainous Tripolis and contemporary and bustling Patra. Every corner of the Peloponnese presents a new challenge. It is one of the most important areas in Greece.

Contents

Foreword 4-5
Geographical position 8

HISTORY 10
Myth and History 10
Mycenean Civilisation 12
The Dorians enter the Peloponnese 13
The 8th century and Colonies ... 14
The century of the Tyrants 15
Sparta Gains the Upper Hand .. 16
The Peloponnesian War 17
4th cent: The Macedonians Arrive 18
The Roman Period 20
The Spread of Christianity 21
The Byzantine Period 22
Frankish Rule 23
Turkish Rule 24
The War of Independence 26
Recent History 27

YESTERDAY AND TODAY
(customs, occupations,
crafts, architecture) 28

A TOUR 39
Itineraries - Map 40-41
KORINTHIA 42
 1. Loutraki 45
 2. Korinth - Ancient Korinth .. 48
 3. Lechaion - Kiato 53
 4. Xylokastro - Stymphalia 55
 5. Korinth - Nemea 58

ARGOLID 60
 6. Ancient Mycenae 64
 7. Argos 69
 8. Argos - Nafplio 70
 9. Nafplio - Tolo - Iria 76
10. Nafplio - Epidaurus 78
11. Epidaurus - Kranidi - Methana 82
12. Argos - Tripoli 85

ARCADIA 86
13. Astros - Leonidi 90
14. Tripoli - Tegea 94
15. Tripoli - Megalopoli 98
16. Megalopoli - A. Karyes 101
17. Megalopoli - Dyrrachi 104

18. Megalopoli - Karytaina 104
19. Tripoli - Astros 106
20. Tripoli - Dimitsana 107
21. Tripoli - Vytina 111
22. Vytina - Langadia 114
23. The Ladonas Dam 115

ACHAÏA 116
24. Diakofto - Kalavryta 119
25. Kalavryta - Tripoli 126
26. Kalavryta - Patra 126
27. Diakofto - Aiyion - Patra .. 127
    Patra 131
28. Patra - Pyrgos 134
29. Patra - Elia 135

ELIA 136
30. Patra - Gastouni 139
31. Amaliada - Pyrgos 143
32. Pyrgos - Olympia 146
    Ancient Olympia 146
33. Pyrgos - Andritsaina 154
34. Loutra Kaïafa - Messinia 158

MESSINIA 160
35. Kyparissia 163
36. Kyparissia - Pylos 164
37. Pylos - Methoni - Koroni .. 170
38. Koroni - Ancient Messene .. 174
    Kalamata 177
39. Kalamata - Kardamyli 180
40. Kalamata - Sparta 183

LACONIA 185
    Sparta 187
    Mystras 191
41. Sparta - Yeraki 196
42. Sparta - Tripoli 197
43. Sparta - Monemvasia 198
44. Mani 205

Map of Archaeological sites
and caves 218
Map of castles and monasteries 219
Geographical particulars 220
Distances (in kilometres) 220
Climatological particulars 221

The Peloponnese is the most southerly part of mainlaind Greece. Its outline resembles a mulberry leaf, which is why its alternative name is the Morea (from the Greece word for mulberry tree), a name which can still be heard today. In 1893, the Peloponnese became —theoretically— an island when the Corinth Canal was opened, breaking through the narrow neck of land which joined the area to the rest of Greece.

Most of the Peloponnese is mountainous. The principal geographical features are the deep gulfs and long capes formed by these mountains in the south and east, and the long, nearly landlocked, Gulf of Corinth in the North.

The principal rock of which the area consists is limestone. Easily eroded and cracked, these limestone deposits have been responsible for a vast variety of natural phenomena, including the internationally famous sea caves at Diros, gorges, swallow-holes, underground rivers and mineral springs.

The mountain chains of the Peloponnese are of the order of 2000 metres in height and are heavily forested, with the expection of those in the south-east and in particilar the hills of the Mani. For most of the year, the hioghest peaks are covered in snow. The ranges run from north to south, and lead down to fertile plains, sandy beaches and pretty bays. The range of natural and geographical conditios in the most important farming areas —such as the valleys or the Pineos in Ilia, the Pamisos in Messinia and the history Eurotas in Lakonia— allow a wide variety of crops to be grown: vegetables, olives and citrus fruit.

The climate of the Peloponnese is Mediterranean, particularly dry and warm on the constline, and continental at higher attitudes, with mild, wet winters. Rainfall is heavier in the west. More natural and geographical particulars can be found in our Useful Information section, on pages 220-221.

CARTE GÉNÉRALE

DE

LA MORÉE ET DES CYCLA

exposant les principaux faits

DE GÉOGRAPHIE ANCIENNE ET DE GÉOGRAPHIE NATUREL

Rédigée au Dépôt général de la Guerre

Par ordre

DE M. LE MARÉCHAL DUC DE DALMATIE

Président du Conseil

A copper engraving of the Peloponnese, produced by the French Mission (1833).

HISTORY

Myth and History

The history of the Peloponnese has beginnings which are lost in the mists of time. As archaeological research progresses, it is constantly pushing back the date of the period in which myth is indistinguishable from history.

The finds in a deep cave at Frangthi (in the Ermioni valley) testify to the presence of populations in this area before 8,000 BC.

Much has been said and written of these first inhabitants of the Peloponnese. These are the stories which survived and came down through the millenia, the legends recorded by Homer, the history written by Herodotus and Thucydides, the raw material for many of the incomparable tragedies of Aeschylus, Sophocles and Euripides.

In the 2nd millenium BC, the Pelasgians were ousted by the Ionians, who settled principally in the north-west of the Peloponnese, by the Aeolians and, above all, by the Achaeans. The Achaeans were skilled and experienced warriors and, as we shall be seeing, they succeeded in founding a strong state and a culture of their own.

Perhaps here, though, we should pause for a moment and see the way in which the myths record the passage of these tribes across the Peloponnese and the way in which they intermingled with each other.

So: the land, as we have said, was inhabited by the Pelasgian tribes, Dryopes, Caucones, Leleges and others. But an invader from Asia Minor conquered them and gave the area his name: this was Pelops, son of Tantalus, king of Sipylos in Phrygia. According to another version, Pelops' father slaughtered his infant son so as to serve him up at a banquet where

the guests were the twelve gods of Olympus. But the gods saw through this disgusting attempt at humour and put Pelops together again, after which, understandably, he left Phrygia and came to the Peloponnese. A third version has Pelops as king of Phrygia: defeated in battle by his next-door neighbour Ilos, founder of Troy (Ilium), he was forced into exile here in Greece. Whatever the reasons for his emigration, the site on which he chose to settle was Pisa, in southern Elis.

Here he discovered a king in residence; this was Oenomaus, who was reluctant to allow his daughter Hippodamia to marry because an oracle had pronounced that he would be killed by his son-in-law. In order to keep prospective suitors at bay, Oenomaus challenged them to a chariot-race, the prize in which was to be Hippodamia's hand. Pelops —with whom, in the meantime Hippodamia had fallen in love— declared that he would take part in the race. With Hip-

podamia's help, he made friends with Myrtilus, Oenomaus' charioteer, whom he persuaded to loosen one of the king's axle-pins. When the race took place, Oenomaus was killed and Pelops married Hippodamia and became king of Elis. The couple had two sons, Atreus and Thyestes, later kings of Mycenae.

At Mycenae, the ruling dynasty to emerge was that of the descendants of Perseus, the founder of the city and son of Zeus and Danae (Danae was a distant descendant of Danaus, who according to earlier myths had come to Greece from Egypt with his daughters). *It was Perseus' grandson Eurystheus who set Heracles, son of Zeus and Alcinia, the twelve feats which he would have to perform to ascend to Mt Olympus as an immortal.*

And so the sons of Pelops, Atreus and Thyestes, came to Mycenae when their father drove them out, and the throne of the city passed into their hands. Afterwards it went to Atreus' son: Agamemnon, conqueror of Troy.

Prehistoric Period - Mycenean Civilisation

With the rise to prominence of the Mycenean civilisation, beginning in about the 16th century BC, we begin to have a fuller knowledge of facts and events in the pre-historic Peloponnese. This was the time about which the Minoan civilisation of Crete began to decline; it was later to be wiped out altogether. It was replaced around the Aegean by the powerful and well-organised military and cultural influence of Mycenae.

Mycenae is the oldest and most famous city-state of the Argolid and in the whole Peloponnese.

Mycenean art: part of a wall-painting from Tiryns (13th century BC).

There was a settlement here well back into the third millenium BC, and when the Achaeans erected their magnificent buildings they used the same site as those who had preceded them.

According to the ancient tales, Mycenae was founded by the mythical hero Perseus, son of Zeus and Danae. After the reign of Eurystheus, the city passed into the hands of its second dynasty, that of the descendants of Pelops. This was the kingly line which was to make Mycenae, with its brilliant civilisation, known all over the ancient world. Agamemnon, grandson of Pelops, was the commander of the Greek forces in the campaign to overcome Troy.

The heights attained by Mycenean civilisation can be seen in the wonderful finds which have come to light there and can be read about in the writings of Greek historians and other ancient sources. The Myceneans were a warlike folk, and even where they could not dominate they made their presence felt throughout the Greek world. And when their military and cultural base was safe and properly organised, they began to spread around the Mediterranean coast, sometimes as the allies of neighbouring peoples (as in the case of the Egyptians) and sometimes on other pretexts (as in the case of the Trojan War).

First as collaborators with the Minoans of Crete and subsequently as their worthy successors, the Achaeans of Mycenae created an entire empire and gathered wealth and power. Between the 16th and the 17th centuries BC they controlled a considerable portion of the known world.

The Dorians enter the Peloponnese

Sometime in the 11th century BC, when Tissamenos was king at Mycenae (he was the son of Orestes and grandson of Agamemnon), a new race of warriors arrived in the Peloponnese: these were the Dorians, and before long they had overthrown Mycenae and taken command of a number of smaller and less important cities as well. Over the centuries which followed, the Dorians captured the Argolid, Corinthia, Laconia and later Messenia. Their principal stronghold was Sparta, which stood on a naturally-fortified site near the fortress of Amyklai and was to become Athens' great enemy in Classical antiquity.

With the rise of Sparta, a struggle for leadership of the Greek world began which was to last centuries. In Arcadia (where the principal cities were Orchomenos, Tegea and Mantineia), the Dorians encountered resistance, while in Messenia, they were swallowed up first by the Achaeans and later by Sparta. Laconia was taken by force, while the earlier enhabitants of the Argolid and Corinthia welcomed their new masters more peacefully. In western Peloponnese, the Aetoloaeolian state of Elis, the ancient Aeolian state of Pisa and the six independent cities of what was later to be called Triphylia continued to survive. The general area of Achaea had already been divided into eastern and western sections; when the Dorians arrived, the Achaeans of Laconia and the Argolid moved west to Aigialeia, which took on the name of Achaea and still bears it today.

The 8th Century and Colonies: History Begins

The most important event in the 8th century was the foundation of colonies by settlers from the Peloponnese, although they were in fact continuing a wave of Greek migration which had begun as early as the 11th century BC.

Another important landmark is to be found in the fact that the 8th century contains the date usually considered to divide prehistory from history: the year 776 BC. This was the year in which the first list of winners of the Olympic Games was drawn up: the first official written monument for posterity. The ancient Greeks, too, counted history from 776, which they recognised as the first Olympic Games.

A krater from the Geometric period, 750 BC.

Archias, a descendent of Heracles, was the first recorded colonist. On the orders of Corinth and Chalkis (the two cities had a kind of commercial alliance), he travelled to Corfu, which he took on behalf of Corinth and where he left Corinthian settlers. Then he sailed across the Adriatic and finally came to Sicily, where in 734 BC he founded the city of Syracuse.

A few years later, in 721 BC, the Achaeans, helped by the city of Troezen, founded the city of Sybaris in southern Italy. It managed to acquire dominance over 27 other cities, while Croton, another city founded about this time by settlers from the Peloponnese, controlled a strip of the Italian peninsula stretching from one side to the other. Thus the Peloponnese has an honourable position in the Greek colonising movement of the 8th century BC, one of significance equal to that held by the bold and restless Ionians of Asia Minor and Euboea.

Back in Greece, war had first broken out between Sparta and Messenia in 743. The First Messenian War (743-724) broke out over the abduction of young Messenians of some Spartan maidens who were attending a feast at the temple of Artemis Limnatis, near the border between the two areas. In reality, however, the cause of the war was the Dorian desire to dominate Messenia.

The art of this period is notable for its geometric decorative motifs, which have caused it to be known as the 'Geometric' period. Among the architectural treasures of the age were the temple of Artemis Orthia at Sparta. Among the archaeological finds from the Geometric period are numerous clay vessels and figurines. The Geometric period, which ended around 700 BC, also saw the use of iron become widespread.

Mycenean vessels decorated with plant and maritime motifs.

The Century of the Tyrants

During the 7th century BC, much of the Peloponnese came to be ruled by tyrants (the dynasty founded by Cypselos in Corinth, for instance, or by Orthagorides in Sikyon). The tyrants supported and revitalised the Olympic Games, continued the establishment of colonies and organised the economy more effectively, developing not only agriculture but manufacturing and trade as well. At the same time, the arts took strides forward. This period, known as the Archaic period, is notable for decorative motifs which what are free and striking by contrast with had gone before. Although continuing to work within the framework of the Doric style, artists began to embellish their creations with the figures of beasts and plants, among other representations. In ar-

chitecture, the heavy style used for the earlier palaces and tombs was abandoned and, although the form was still Doric, temples grew lighter (among examples are that of Apollo in Corinth and of Hera at Olympia). There were particularly important developments in sculpture, with famous workshops at Corinth, Argos and Sikyon. Corinth and Sikyon set the pace in painting, too, along with the artists of Cleonai and Laconia.

Throughout the century there was constant fighting between the earlier inhabitants of the Peloponnese and the more recent arrivals (Dorians) for control over the wider geographical area. Argos, whose ruling house claimed to be the descendants of the Myceneans and to continue their traditions, managed, under their king and military commander Pheidon, to defeat Sparta. According to an ancient tradition, Pheidon was the first 15

The two faces of a coin from Argos (370-330 BC).

ruler in the Peloponnese (and according to another version, in the whole of Greece) to mint coins and to set up a system of weights and measures.

The courts of the tyrants and the general economic well-being favoured the development of a vigorous tradition in literature; local writers were active and the Peloponnese also attracted authors from elsewhere. The leading figures in 7th century literature included Tyrtaeus, a Laconian poet whose elegies inspired the Spartans during the Second Messenian War, Arion, who lived at the court of the tyrant Periander of Corinth and gave the dithyramb theatrical form, the epic poet Eumelos of Corinth and Sakadas, a musician and poet from Argos.

The Second Messenian War began in 645, with a revolt organised by Aristomenes from Andania, who brought out Arcadia, Argos and Sikyon against Sparta. Fighting continued until 628, when the Spartans defeated the Messenians - who had, however, been betrayed by the Arcadians.

The Messenians took refuge in the fortress of Eira and Aristomenes fell into the hands of the Spartans, who cast him into the Caiadas Gorge. However, by a near-miracle he managed to survive and fled to Messenia to carry on the fight. When the castle of Eira eventually fell —once more by treason— Aristomenes fled again, to Arcadia. The rest of the Messenian population was enslaved by Sparta, as helots. But Aristomenes' children, with quite a number of Messenians —most of them from Pylos and Methone— set sail for Sicily, where they occupied the city of Zagkle and renamed it Messene. Back in Messenia, the war was followed by some two and a half centuries of depopulation and decline.

The 6th Century: Sparta Gains the Upper Hand

By the early 6th century, the ruling dynasty in Sikyon was losing control of the city and its surroundings and had been particularly weakened by a 'holy war' which the tyrant Cleisthenes had waged on behalf of Delphi between 600 and 590. Thus, after the defeat of Messenia, a new period began in which parts of the Peloponnese came under Spartan domination or were forced to enter into alliance with it.

Sikyon was the first to be beaten; Sparta then forced Tegea to sign a treaty of support. Pisa was soon destroyed, and an understanding was reached with Corinth (Sparta and Corinth then proceeded to fail in an expedition against the tyrant Polycrates of Samos). Parts of the Argolid were occupied by Spartans.

The power and fame of Sparta grew, and it could now be said that the city was the focus of power in the Peloponnese. Its development took place in parallel to and up to the same level as the other leading city in Greece at the time, Athens.

The 5th Century: the Persian Wars and the Peloponnesian War

The opening decades of the 5th century were marked by the Persian Wars. After suppressing the revolt in the Ionian cities of Asia Minor (499-494), the Persians embarked on an attempt to conquer Greece proper. In 490, Darius led his forces into mainland Greece. Athens, asked for help from Sparta, seeing in the Asian armies a threat which menaced the whole of the Greek world. Yet when the decisive battle came, at Marathon, the Athenians stood alone, with the help of a few soldiers from Plataeae. The Spartans were unable to come, they said; they were celebrating the important feast of the Carneia. A detachment of 2,000 men —all that could be spared, they said— arrived in Athens to find the Athenians celebrating their triumph over the enemy from the east.

Ten years later, the Persians were back, under Xerxes this time. During this second campaign, the Spartans and other Peloponnesians took part in all the major battles, fighting side-by-side with the Athenians and men from other cities. The heroic sacrifice of the Spartan king Leonidas and his three hundred men, at Thermopylae in 480 BC, has gone down in human history as one of the supreme acts of self-immolation. After holding up the huge Persian army for four whole days, Leonidas and his men were outflanked when a traitor showed the invaders a mountain path. Abandoned by the rest of the tiny Greek force, Leonidas' three hundred and a small group of Thespians were slaughtered to the last man. Later in the campaign, the Spartans and other Peloponnesians were to fight bravely by the side of the other Greeks in the victorious battles of Salamis (480) and Plataeae (479).

Almost as soon as the common enemy had been driven off, the quarrels and rivalries broke out in Greece once again. The most powerful cities attempted to impose their rule on the others, while the weaker city-states sought desperately for the most promising and safest alliance. The shift away from oligarchy and towards democracy gained momentum in the Peloponnesse, and its main success was the establishment of a democratic system in Elis.

At Thermopylae, where the Spartans fell in heroic combat, stands a statue of Leonidas with the famous epigram of Simonides:

«῍Ω ξεῖν ἀγγέλλειν Λακεδαιμονίοις, ὅτι τῇδε κείμεθα τοῖς κείνων ῥήμασι πειθόμενοι».

"Go and tell the Spartans, thou that paessest by,
That here, obedient to their laws, we lie".

In 464 BC, Sparta was totally flattened by a terrible earthquake which is said to have killed as many as 20,000 people. The Messenians seized the opportunity to declare war on their ancient rivals, and ten years of fighting ensued. In the end, Sparta was victorious once more and many Messenians were forced to take refuge in Naupactus.

More wars followed: Corinth, Epidaurus and Aegina against Athens in 458-457, Sparta and Thebes against Athens and Argos in 456. The decisive confrontation was approaching.

Despite all the diplomatic efforts made between 446 and 431 and the peace agreement reached between Sparta and Athens, the two cities were unable to put a stop to the disputes which were constantly breaking out between their allies. Matters went from bad to worse, and in 432 trouble affected the diplomatic level as well, leading in 431 to the outbreak of what was known as the Peloponnesian War. In effect, this was a conflict between one half of the Greek world and the other, since both Athens and Sparta enlisted the assistance of powerful allied forces. The Peloponnesian War ended in 404 with victory for Sparta, but 27 years of fighting had led to serious losses in terms both of manpower and resources. The war left a heritage of depopulation, of a weakening of the Greek world, of acute political contradictions and of a break in cultural and economic development.

The 4th Century: the Macedonians Arrive

The late 5th and early 4th centuries found Sparta at war with Elis (the war began in 401) and subjecting its inhabitants. Now the rulers of Sparta, drunk on victory and power, looked around for ever more impressive conquests.

In 399 they undertook a campaign against Persia, with Thibron and (later) Derkylis as their generals. Three years later a fresh Spartan expeditionary force left for Asia Minor, under Agesilaus. The Persians faced a serious threat in these campaigns, which were known as the Ionian War, and to rid themselves of the Spartans fomented the Corinthian War in 395, which caused the recall of Agesilaus.

The Corinthians, grown fat and rebellious on the spoils of the Peloponnesian War, allied themselves with Athens, Argos, Euboea, Locris, Leucas, Acarnania and Thessaly and, in 394, convened a conference in Corinth for the purpose of organising an attack on Sparta. With the help of Tegea, Sparta fell on the conference and beat the surprised allied troops. But at about the same time, the Spartan fleet was defeated off Cnidus by the Athenian fleet under Conon (which had the assistance of Persian triremes) and, together with half its vessels, Sparta lost control of the Greek seas.

Although the campaign against Sparta had to be called off, the fighting in the Corinthian War —which was fanned by Persia— focused around Corinth, while at the same time nearly all the Aegean islands and coastal states threw off the Spartan yoke. Before long, the growing strength of the (second) 'Athenian League' began to alarm the Persians, who changed tack and attempted to reach an agreement with Sparta.

In the end, the 'Peace of An-

A coin of the times of King Philip.

talcidas' —so damaging for Hellenism as a whole— was signed, and Sparta handed over to the Persians the Greek cities of Asia Minor, in exchange for (questionable) recognition of its leading role in Greek domestic affairs.

Before long, reaction mounted and Thebes, the rising power in Greece, began to challenge Sparta openly.

At the battle of Leuctra Thebes defeated Sparta and went on to organise and carry out four campaigns in the Peloponnese (370-362), which ended with the complete subjugation of Laconia and the recognition of Thebes as the leading city in Greek affairs. The Thebans built Megalopolis and Messene on the borders of Sparta and managed to maintain their hold over the Peloponnese and Greece in general until the death of their leader Epaminondas, who was killed at the battle of Mantineia in 362.

Around the middle of the 4th century the new power in the Greek north, the Macedonians, began to extend their influence southwards through mainland Greece.

Philip of Macedon gained a voice in the affairs of the Peloponnese in 342, when he took Elis, Megalopolis, Messene and Argos under his protection. After the battle of Chaironeia, the Macedonians stormed through the Peloponnese and left Laconia in ruins. In this campaign, they had Argos, Arcadia and Messene as their allies.

In Corinth, the assembled representatives of the cities which formed the Corinthian Alliance recognised Philip as commander-in-chief for the campaign against Persia which was to follow and proclaimed the independence of all the Greek cities.

Alexander the Great, who soon succeeded his father Philip, was also recognised as commander for the Persian campaign. This is not the place to go into detail about Alexander's conquests; suffice it to say that while he was on the throne a revolt, under Ages, broke out in the Peloponnese against Macedonian rule. Alexander's forces put down the revolt and killed Ages.

After Alexander's death, the infighting and personal rivalries of his successors extended to the Peloponnese, where the first conflict between the opposing camps took place.

In 303 BC, Demetrius Poliorcetes, who had conquered almost all the Peloponnese in a single campaign, was recognised as commander-in-chief of all the Greeks.

The 3rd Century: the Achaean League

During the early 3rd century disputes and conflicts continued between the Macedonians (Antigonids), the Spartans and a third federal power in the Peloponnese, the Achaean League. This confederation of the Achaean cities of the Peloponnese was originally founded in the 8th century BC and was re-instituted in 280, on a different basis. The initial participants were the cities of Dyme, Patrae, Tritaea and Pharae, with other Achaean cities joining at a later date. After some years, the power of the Achaean League spread through almost all the Peloponnese.

When the Spartan king Cleomenes threatened to make war on the Achaean League, Aratus, the League's general, sought help from Macedon. King Antigonus Doson was only too willing to provide such assistance: it gave him a pretext for intervening in the Peloponnese. Sparta was defeated at the battle of Sellasia and Macedon had the Peloponnese in its hands once more. A Macedonian garrison was installed at Corinth.

In the closing years of the 3rd century, after the death of Cleomenes, Sparta underwent a number of strange mishaps at the hands of various adventurers, and there were repeated interventions by the Achaean League and its adversary the Aetolian League.

In the meantime, the Romans had been preparing for their invasion of Greece and their intervention in the friction and clashes between Greek forces.

The Roman Period

Although Philip III of Macedon was victorious in the First Macedonian War and had forced the Romans to sign a peace treaty in 205, a fresh war between Rome and Macedon broke out in 200-197. Titus Quinctius Flamininus, the Roman commander, managed to bring almost all the Greek cities into alliance with him: the Romans, it was believed, would rid southern Greece of the Macedonians. At the battle of Cynoscephalae, in Thessaly, the Romans defeated the Macedonians and then embarked on a campaign of absorbing the rest of Greece piecemeal. In the Peloponnese, there were two camps, broadly speaking: one which favoured the Romans and one which opposed them. The Romans alternately diminished and exploited the power of the Achaean League in order to spread dissent among the cities of the Peloponnese. In the end, after a combination of diplomatic manoeuvring and shows of force, the Roman consul Lucius Mummius defeated the army of the Achaean League near Leucopetra in 146, and entered Corinth in triumph. He razed the city, killed all its men, carried the women and children off into slavery and took most of the city's artistic treasures back to Italy with him. He then marched through the Peloponnese, demolishing the walls of other cities and annexing it, together with the rest of Greece, to the Roman province of Macedonia.

The Romans rebuilt and strengthened Corinth, particularly in the time of Julius Caesar. The city flourished once more, in both commerce and the arts.

Part of an icon of St Andrew (1846) from the Cathedral of Patra.

The Appearance and Spread of Christianity

In 52 AD St Paul arrived in Corinth. He realised immediately that if he could manage to found a Christian church in this populous city, with its commercial power and its two harbours for communications, then the religion of love would soon spread throughout Greece.

Reaction was not long in appearing, however, and St Paul was brought before the Roman commander of the city, in the centre of the Agora. He decided that St Paul's teaching was not illegal and released him; soon there was a Christian church in Corinth.

As long as St Paul stayed in Corinth, the church there was a model of order and morals. But within four years of his departure, the problems had begun to multiply and it was essential that St Paul should intervene. From Ephesus and Philippi he wrote his two Epistles to his Corinthian brethren, in which he emphasises that Christians do not belong to persons, political parties, or factions, but to the great Christian family. All are brothers, and in the souls of all Christ reigns with His infinite love. Paul's Epistles are exhortations for unity, for love; he counsels true wisdom, the sanctity of the body, justice, freedom to live in peace and the maximum exploitation of personal gifts.

By now St Paul's work had sent down roots. The dissemination of Christianity throughout the world was merely a matter of time, and Corinth became one of the three most important centres for the spread of the new religion across the Peloponnese: the others were Patra (where St Andrew was martyred) and Sparta.

The Byzantine Period

Laid waste by the warfare and looting of the Roman period, the Peloponnese was slow to take the road of recovery and reconstruction. Its distance from the seat of the Byzantine Empire and its poverty-stricken depopulation meant that in the early Byzantine period little attention was paid to it.

On the other hand, its geographical position and the fact that it had no organised military protection meant that it was wide open to attack from barbarians and pirates.

Between the 7th and the 11th centuries the Peloponnese was a separate administrative region within the Byzantine Empire (such regions were known as 'themes'). Corinth was its capital, and continued to be after the 11th century, when the region was re-named 'The Theme of Greece' and eastern central Greece was included within it. Among the cities which stood out and flourished in Byzantine times were Corinth, Patra, Argos, Nafplio, Monemvasia. Lakedaimonia Vostinza (Egeo), Methoni and Koroni.

Later in the 13th century, the star of Mystras was in the ascendant. This superb city, capital of the Despotate of the Morea and birthplace of the last Byzantine Emperor, boasted 40,000 inhabitants at its height. It was the cradle of the neo-Platonism of Gemistus Plethon (who made a major contribution to the Renaissance in Western Europe) and its school of icon-painting was famed throughout the Christian world. Mystras was sometimes called 'the Florence of the East'.

Mystras: a wall-painting from the Pantanassa ('Queen of the World') convent.

Nafplio: a copper engraving 1830 (G.N. Wright: The Rhine, Italy and Greece in Drawings).

Frankish Rule

After conquering Central Greece, the 'Frankish' forces of King Boniface of Thessaloniki ('Frankish' is the blanket term used in Greece to describe the Catholic, Western European marauders who ruled much of Greece in the Middle Ages) moved south to occupy the Peloponnese almost without resistance. By 1212, the Franks held the whole region, with the exception of Monemvasia, Methoni and Koroni.

The Greeks of the Peloponnese did not look favourably on their foreign conquerors and seized every opportunity that presented itself to react to their administration and their evident desire to grab whatever they could lay hands on. In the 13th century, the Byzantine Emperor Michael Palaeologus re-took Constantinople for the Empire and then captured William de Villehardouin in Pelagonia; in order to obtain his release, de Villehardouin promised to liberate some parts of the Peloponnese. And so in 1262 the two beautiful Byzantine cities of Mystras and Monemvasia were returned to the Empire, together with a substantial part of the south-eastern Peloponnese.

This period was followed by one of renewed depopulation and looting of the Peloponnese on the part of Catalan and Turkish pirates and freebooters.

To keep out these brigands, the Six-Mile Wall across the Isthmus at Corinth was re-built, with 153 towers. But even it failed to hold up the Turkish rabble of Turahan, who invaded the Peloponnese in 1423, destroying many cities and looting the area.

In 1430, the Empire signalled the end of Frankish rule in the Peloponnese by abolishing the Catholic arch bishopric of Patra. After this, only Methoni, Koroni, Argos and Nafplio remained in Venetian hands.

23

Turkish Rule

For many centuries, the Turks had been calculating the benefits to be obtained from an occupation of the Peloponnese. Their occasional presence in the area —as pirates or brigands— gave them still more of an opportunity to appreciate the peninsula's potential.

Now, however, the Turkish threat had become more specific. When Sultan Murat II in person headed the Ottoman forces, the royal Palaeologus family was defeated and forced to recognise Turkish suzerainty. In 1449 Constantine Palaeologus went to Constantinople, where he became the last Emperor of Byzantium (he was killed during the fall of Constantinople in 1453).

The two remaining Palaeologus brothers, Thomas and Demetrius, split the Peloponnese up between themselves, but a fresh Turkish invasion, under Turahan and his son Ahmet, succeeded in occupying the peninsula as far as Messenia in the west and Megalopolis in the centre. When Constantinople fell, the Albanians of Arcadia, under Petros Bouas rose in revolt, and the leader of the Greeks of the Mani, Manuil Katakouzinos, declared his independence from the rump of the Empire. The two Palaeologus brothers were forced to call in the Turks, of all people, to keep themselves in power. The Turks were only too happy to oblige, of course, but in return the Palaeologus brothers had to declare themselves tributaries of the Sultan. Before long, however, they were unable to keep up the payments of tribute and the Turks, under Sultan Mohammed II, carried out two campaigns in the Peloponnese. During the first of these, in 1458, the Palaeologus brothers were able to defend themselves in the fortresses of Mantineia and Monemvasia, but when the Turks returned two years later Demetrius was

The atmosphere of secrecy

forced to surrender Mystras and Thomas fled to Italy.

The centuries which followed were a period of struggles for freedom, vicious reprisals, epidemics and invasions.

As early as the late 16th century, there were bands of free Greeks —usually described as 'armatoli and klephts', which means armed men and robbers— in the mountains of the Peloponnese. Their raids on the Turks

The 'hidden school' is conveyed in unique manner in this painting by Gyzis.

were a constant nuisance to the Ottoman authorities, and they passed on to coming generations a tradition of bravery and an example of resistance.

Seeing the power of these bands, the Turks waged constant war on them. Many men from the Peloponnese were forced to take refuge in the Ionian Islands, where they received proper military training in the French and British occupying forces.

Throughout this period of slavery, Christianity continued to be the spiritual bulwark of the population, keeping alive the dream of freedom until the War of Independence began in 1821.

The tradition of Greek learning was kept alive in the 'secret schools' run by the priests, where generations of Greeks of the Peloponnese received their education.

The War of Independence: Liberation

In the early 19th century, the vision of an organised liberation movement began to transform itself into specific proposals and plans. The idea of a specific War of Independence took shape first among the Greeks who lived outside the country. They founded the Society of Friends ('Philike Hetereia'), which gathered the first funds, made the first arrangements, organised the first armed units and started the fight outside Greece proper. On 25 March 1821, the Greeks raised the banner of liberation at the Megisti Lavra Monastery, in the northern Peloponnese. With Theodoros Kolokotronis as their commander-in-chief, the Greeks turned the whole of the Peloponnese into a theatre of war. In the first year of the revolution, the capture of Tripolitsa (Tripoli) gave the cause strong foundations. In the second, the battle of Dervenakia and the annihilation of the Turkish forces under Dramalis constituted a major achievement. It was in the Peloponnese that the first national assembly took place in 1821, to give the war-torn country its first semblance of democratic organisation. This meeting was followed by the National Assemblies of Epidaurus in 1822 and of Astros in 1823, which drew up formal constitutional principles. The naval battle of Navarino marked the final triumph over the Turks, and in 1828 Ioannis Capodistias arrived in Greece to serve as the country's first governor.

On 25 March 1821 Bishop Germanos of Palaia Patra raised the banner of freedom at the Ayia Lavra Monastery and swore in the revolutionaries.

The battle of Navarino as painted by P. Zografos on the instructions of General Makriyannis.

Recent History

Nafplio became the first capital of the new Greek state, and it was there that Capodistrias was assassinated in 1831.

The reign of King Othon began in the Peloponnese too, with the work of the Regents appointed until he came of age. And the Peloponnese was also the scene of the first anti-Othonian demonstrations.

Between 1843 and 1852 there were frequent agrarian uprisings in the Peloponnese.

The development of light industry, heavy industry and larger towns and cities was accompanied by the spread of a anarchist movement, which first manifested itself in Patra in 1877 and had spread to the western Peloponnese by 1896. There was more agrarian unrest in the period after 1902.

In the meantime, the Peloponnese railway had been constructed in 1880 and the region was developing closer and closer ties with the rest of Greece. From this period on, the history of the Peloponnese is that of Greece as a whole.

The Peloponnese has given Greece some of its most important political leaders and large numbers of civil servants.

During the Second World War and the German occupation, the Peloponnese was the scene of decisive battles between the Greek resistance movement and the occupying forces.

The total destruction of Kalavryta by German troops marks out in the most tragic manner the contribution which the Greeks of the Peloponnese have made to the cause of building a world of peace and freedom between peoples and nations, in the spirit of ancient Olympia and the Olympic ideal, in the spirit of the brotherhood of man.

YESTERDAY AND TODAY

And they called it the Peloponnese, the land of Pelops, mythical king of Pisa. The people who have lived there, from pre-historic times to the present, have created in this land the most diverse forms of culture. This land has known many moments of greatness, many of the ups and downs of history. Things have changed often in this peninsula - a peninsula which became, in effect, an island when the Corinth Canal was dug through the Isthmus in 1893.

Today, as we approach the dawn of yet another century, the 21st since the birth of Christ, the Peloponnese, with its mythical name, hums with life, with a vast variety of different activities: farming and factories, stock-breeding, fishing, commercial enterprises of every imaginable sort, universities, tourism.

Modern development has meant that the characteristics which the Peloponnese now shares with the rest of Greece are numerous. Despite that, the old question still remains topical: what is it that makes someone feel 'a Peloponnesian'? And do the people of this area really feel that their first loyalty is to the Peloponnese and afterwards to the Mani, Kalamata, Pyrgos, Patra or Tripoli? Why, when asked where they come from, do the Peloponnesians reply proudly that they were born 'south of the ditch', meaning the Corinth Canal? What is the meaning of all this? It means that, on the hand, we have to aknowledge of the particular features which the varying geographical conditions and historical circumstances have given to each separate area of 'Old Greece'. Picture the inhabitants of upland Arkadia next to those of Kalamata or

of Pylos, whose gaze rests daily on the blue waters of the Messenian Gulf. Or imagine the farmers of the Argolic plain or the rich fields of Elia with the hardy mountaineers of Taygetos. On the other hand, though, differences in occupation, customs and habits have not prevented the development of an awareness in all these people that they share a common fate, a fate which they themselves have created as they walk the paths of history. They belong to a famous land, an entity with an invaluable cultural heritage. Their traditions are bound up with modern life and reality; they are not just piles of famous ruins. The people who live in the Peloponnese do not just run their lives a few miles from the remains of Golden Mycenae, or outside the perimeter fence at Ancient Olympia, or near the Byzantine city of Mystras, or even inside the walls of the wonderful castles of Monemvasia and Koroni. The children who are born in this part of Greece learn, along with the other stories, about the Venetian knights who, on horseback and clad in armour, issue forth from Methoni castle at dead of night to claim the glory that once was theirs.

Those children learn that to dive off the golden beaches of Elia is to see the sunken ruins of the ancient city of Letrina, or that for centuries now the beautiful princess Catherine Palaiologushas haunted the Castle 'tis Orias' near Kalavryta, from whose walls she threw herself so as not to fall into Turkish hands.

This is not to say, of course, that the people of the Peloponnese are Dorians in blue jeans. No Pelasgians or Myceneans stalk the streets of Corinth or Patra. The passing centuries have brought to the Peloponnese very many people from other parts of the Greek world: for example, the thousands of refugees who arrived after the defeat of Greece in the war of 1922 with Turkey, the campaign usually known as the Asia Minor disaster. And there have been influxes of populations from outside the Greek world, too, who left their traces here. Yet there has also been movement of population outward, often, in the past, in search of refuge from the murderous hand of an occupying enemy. In 1769, for example, the people of the Peloponnese rose in rebellion against the Turks, spurred on by the Orloff brothers, emissaries of Catherine the Great of Russia. When the revolt failed, 80,000 Peloponnesians fled to the coasts of Asia Minor.

There have been changes, too, which stemmed from internal migration, within the boundaries of the Peloponnese; such movements were usually for economic reasons. Until recently, there was a trend for the villagers of the Peloponnese to come down to live in the towns and cities which were growing. For many young people, too, the towns and cities were a natural goal. Even today, there are many people who set out from Athens to return to the family home in the Mani, perhaps, or near Kalamata, to help bring in the olive crop. And there are thousands more who, in the early 20th century, went further afield, to America or Australia, to seek their fortunes.

For all that, the people who live in the Peloponnese today, leading lives changed as we have described above, inhabit towns and villages whose names may go back to the ancient gods, such as Tyros in Arkadia, whose name is derived from the temple of Apollo Tyrites which once stood there, or Areopolis, from Ares, the god of war. Although the population today is uniformly Greek, some of the placenames are of Slavic origin,

An ancient vessel (520 BC) showing the harvesting of olives in a manner little different from that practised today.

such as Zatouna (= 'over the river') or Stemnitsa (= 'rocky gorge'). They worship in churches which have kept their non-Greek names, such as the Oblou monastery in Patra, whose name comes from the Albanian word 'obile', which means sweet. In some cases they remind one of the words of the great modern Greek poet George Seferis:

"They acted like the trees and the waves - which bend to the wind and the rain - which bend to the night and the sun - in change, without changing".

That is particularly the case in the south east Peloponnese, at Leonidio in Arkadia, where they still speak Tsakonian, a version of the ancient Doric dialect.

In his 'Everyday Life in Mycenean Times' Paul Faure notes that:

"The contemporaries of Odysseus and Agamemnon bequeathed to the Greeks of the first millenium before Christ a certain number of imperishable commodities - ones which have come down to us, as well. I am not talking here of the gold face-masks of Mycenae, which in my opinion are ugly rather than the reverse, and of which the whole world was to be entirely ignorant until 1876. They bequeathed something which will last longer than all the furbelows on all the skirts, than all the jewellery in their tombs, than all their lengthy wooden triremes, than all their pottery of baked clay and even of bronze, and even longer than those huge, those amazing stone acropoleis: a spirit - that is, ideas, inventions, ethics. And above all, they bequeathed a religious, political, judicial, technical and military vocabulary which is still in use. How can one fail to remember, among a thousand other examples, the word 'theos' for God, the word 'demos' for the source of popular power, 'tekton' for ar-
chitect, 'iater' for doctor? The praises of those to whom no homage was paid, the hymns they sang over their tombs, stimulated the imaginations of the epic poets and later of the tragedians; the Classical theatre was born out of the living dramas of Thebes, Tiryns and Argos.

Mycenean Greece laid up a treasurehouse of examples which even their most distant descendants made use of. These men and women, who were once personalities, became characters, types of passionate warriors. They knew well that their fate had been decided in advance; but nonetheless they liked great danger, wagers, fighting, even sporting contests in honour of the dead. Their descendants retained that inclination perpetually.

Where else can be the root of the love which the Greeks still have for open debate, for the juxtaposition of ideas, for struggle and competition, if not from an age in which the bold called authority into question, travelled, discovered other countries and other heroes? Oedipus, Heracles, Jason, Odysseus: these self-made and self-confident men believed they could overcome all the monsters, the Sphinx, the Hydra, the Dragon or Proteus, by relying on human willpower. Their distant descendants never forgot the lesson they taught: 'There are many wonders in the world', said Sophocles, 'but nothing more wonderful than man'. One of the rarest gifts of the heroes of the Trojan War was, perhaps, that they believed not in wisdom but in human action".

The people of the Peloponnese are restless, active, and creative even in the most difficult conditions: it it should not be forgotten that they managed to extricate themselves from the insignificance which followed the Roman occupation of the

Peloponnese and from the relative depopulation which resulted from the imposition of Turkish rule.

As well as the educational level of its people, the development of the region can be attributed to economic factors. For the last four hundred years, the basic occupations of the people of the Peloponnese have been agricultural. The fields of the farmers ran back into the hinterland, to the foothills of the mountains; and further up, the shepherds ran their flocks on the slopes of Mt Parnon, Mt Mainalon and Mt Taygetos. There were artisans, too, who made thick cloth, silk and silken materials, furs, cotton, and threads dyed white or red which were much sought-after on the markets of Western Europe.

They laid the foundations for the light and heavy industry of the present, for the engineering plants, the

For all the technical advances made in farming, horse-drawn ploughs will still be seen today in smaller villages.

cotton and thread mills, the paper-mills, the olive presses, the currant processing factories and all the other units.

The people of the Peloponnese were outstanding merchants, too. They began in the 17th century with five or six ships, and a century later they had several hundreds. Just before the outbreak of the War of Independence, in 1821, their exports to Western Europe were worth more than 4 million francs.

The tradition in the transit trade begun then still continues today, and some of the cities of the Peloponnese, such as Corinth, Patra and Kalamata, are among the leading Greek commercial centres.

They were skilled craftsmen, too, though they often had to travel in search of clients. They would spend the winter in the mountain villages of the Peloponnese and, come the spring, set out with the tools of their trade to work in towns and villages all over Greece. Often they went in gangs, whole teams of workmen. The barrel-makers of Pyrgos, in Elia, were known throughout the country, while the goldsmiths of Stemnitsa would work their rings and jewellery seated on their donkeys as the beasts plodded along. Some of the best-known jewellers in Athens today are descendants of these travelling goldsmiths and continue to practise their skills. There were wood-carvers from Valtesiniko, and builders from Langadia who would undertake structures of any kind at all: houses, churches, towers, fountains, even arched bridges. Each team of men consisted of between ten and twenty masons, plus a retinue of apprentices and assistants. The whole team was managed by a foreman and would include all the necessary specialisations: stone-masons, quarrymen, plasterers, carpenters, wood-carvers, painters.

The architecture of the houses they built took into account the natural surroundings, the environment and the needs created by the occupations of the people who would live in them. Thus, in low-lying areas (where the villages, at that time, belonged to large estates), the houses were usually single-storey and built of brick with a wooden frame or supporting beams. In the coastal parts of the southern Peloponnese these houses are painted even today in bright and lively colours. In the mountain areas the houses were built of stone and were almost invariably two-storeyed.

On the ground floor (the 'katoi'), would be the byre for the larger animals, with their feeding-troughs, the wine and cheese barrels, and a loft for seed crops. In the low-lying areas this byre or barn was a separate building.

The upper storey (the 'anoi') was reached by an outside staircase on the eastern side, leading to a covered balcony (the 'hayiati'). Inside would be the parlour and the bedrooms, with a fireplace on the blind north wall.

Roofs were usually gabled and were covered with slates or tiles which had to be strong enough to cope with the heavy snows of winter. Old stone houses of this type, with tiled roofs, can be seen in Andritsaina and elsewhere. Very often, these houses had no internal partitions. The 'open-plan' parlour, living-room and other areas were indications of prosperity and we encounter them in areas where the local architectural style was more complex.

The general impression of these villages, as they come in sight from a distance, is most attractive, particularly where the natural setting is beautiful as well and there are woods or beaches. Yet when one enters the village one is often disappointed; this should not surprise us, for there is a harmonious relationship between the village and its environment, which by itself is often striking and interesting, thus drawing the eye from the village and absorbing many of its imperfections.

In recent years, the State has declared many of these villages to be historic monuments and forbidden new buildings in them (the Peloponnese has the majority of such settlements throughout Greece). Private enterprise has played its part, too, in their restoration. This also applies to the towers and tower-houses of the Mani, a separate and very different note in the architecture of the Peloponnese. These stone structures played a number of roles: they were houses and fortresses simultaneously, designed to protect the family and its property and keep out would-be invaders. In the cities which grew into industrial and commercial centres in the early 20th century, a large number of houses and public buildings were designed in the neo-Classical style, notably by the Bavarian architect Ziller. Ziller came to Greece with King Othon (who was also a Bavarian), and among his work in Patra are the church of the Purification of the Virgin, the Old Market, the Municipal Library and the Theatre, which is a copy of La Scala in Milan. All over the Peloponnese, in villages and towns, the people built their daily lives along with their houses, incorporating their joys and sorrows, giving solid form to their beliefs, their values - a whole moral world which has not disappeared because, among other things, it was reflected in their arts, which even today still tell us of the people who lived, loved, struggled and believed there.

The fundamental expression of painting in the Peloponnese in modern times —that is, since the Byzantine period— has been icon-painting. Since the 10th century, hundreds of churches have been decorated with murals and portable icons of the saints. Most of the artists are anonymous, with some rare exceptions, such as Dimitris Moschos of Nafplio, who in the early 17th century painted the murals for the Monastery of Our Lady 'Aimyalous'. Panayiotis Zografos, another Peloponnesian painter, was from Sparta. Although not a painter by profession, he became the artist of the War of Independence. He fought with General Makriyannis and was commissioned by him to illustrate his memoirs. For this project he produced 25 oil-paintings on wood showing scenes from the War and the first 25 years of independence.

However, wood was normally used for carving in the Peloponnese. Valtesiniko has the greatest tradition in producing these marvellous works of art, and it was the home village of the Dinopoulos brothers, who carved the highly ornate screen in the church of the Sts Theodore in the vicinity. Throught out the Peloponnese fine work is done in the carving

The screen in the church of the New Monastery of Ayia Lavra (1850).

of walnut, which is often gilted afterwards. Old wood carving is often to be found in the interiors of the houses, particularly in mountain areas; the carved ceilings of the houses in upland Arkadia are especially fine.

Wood was also used, of course, for everyday purposes: to make furniture, domestic utensils, the distinctive stamps which were impressed into every loaf of bread before baking. Shepherds would carve their crooks as they sat alone watching the flocks, or distaffs, spoons or pipes. In Karyraina they made wooden goblets, which were then painted in lively colours - red, perhaps, or green.

Today, most wood-carving is done to produce souvenirs for tourists, but in their day such items were an inseparable part of the everyday life of farmers and shepherds. The same is true of pottery. The Peloponnese never had a particularly strong individual style in pottery, though much was made, especially in the Patra area and in Messinia. The villages of Vounaria and Petrades and the district to the north of Koroni were famous for their 'tzares', huge, heavy jars (the words are related, through Italian) in which farmers kept their harvested crops. In 1955 there were 30 workshops turning out these jars; now there is only one.

Otherwise, pottery was used to make numerous domestic utensils and containers: basins in which the women kneaded the dough for the bread or the special ring-shaped loaves for weddings and Easter, flowerpots, bowls, water-jugs, cups, and many other items.

Making bread was not the women's only task, of course; they made a major contribution to the day-to-day chores in the house and in the fields, as well as helping to tend

the animals. There were, however, jobs which were reserved only for women: they spun the wool and cotton and wove the cotton cloth which was widely used in the household. Sometimes, too, they would make silken shirts.

In quieter moments, the women loved to embroider. Here again silk was used, with thread of the liveliest colours and complex designs in which the favourite motifs were roses and the branches of vines, olives and myrtles. The reputation for embroidery of some areas was so great that songs were made about it, as in the case of Kalamata and its kerchiefs, a song which is still common today.

Today it is a rare sight to see a woman embroidering or weaving. Some bread is still baked, particularly on special occasions, but sewing is a spare-time activity and is practised more among the elderly than the young.

For the men, leisure activities have not changed: they centre around the coffee-shop, with backgammon and the card-game 'prefa' to while away the time.

There are some customs and habits which have died out altogether in the cities and live on only in the smallest villages. Many of these customs were of great cultural importance in the past; one of them was the evening gathering in the 'rouga', the centre of the village. There the man would talk over the problems facing the community and the women would tell their tales of childbirth, marriage and work. There, too, the children would learn the traditional games and sports.

On the other hand, there are also customs and practices which have been handed down intact from one generation to another.

One of these is music, and particularly song. The favourite instruments in the Peloponnese were the various sizes and pitches of wooden flutes and recorders, the 'santouri' (rather like a zither), the lute, the drum and the tambourine. In more recent times, under Western influence, the violin was added, but the manner in which it is played owes nothing at all to the Classical tradition. In the 19th century the clarinet was added to the band, and gradually displaced the bagpipe, which had dominated until then. The self-taught folk musicians would form miniature orchestras, with perhaps a violin and a lute or two bagpipes and a drum. Today, the most common composition of such bands is violin, lute, clarinet and santouri.

The instrumental music is usually played by the band as a whole. Individual pieces are rarer, and are normally confined to improvisations for the clarinet with the drum beating out the background rhythm. The songs of the Peloponnese, which are the most common musical form of all, cover every possible aspect of human life. There are 'songs of the table', which are never danced to, and dance songs, which accompany the steps of the dance. The dance songs of the Peloponnese are majestic and a little formal by comparison with those of Macedonia, for instance, which are more lively. On holidays and feast-days, the dance song will accompany the three favourite dances, the kalamatianos, the tsakonikos and the tsamikos. The kalamatianos in danced throughout Greece; it is circular and the dancers form a chain. As can be seen from its name, it originated in the Peloponnese. The tsakonikos has a whole history of its own. Originating in Tsakonika, which is part of the province of Kynouria, it consists of a line

At feasts folk dancing is a demonstration of manhood and festive mood.

of dancers who wheel tightly round each other and then swing free in strange spiral patterns. This greatly resembles the dance described by the ancient writers as the 'geranos'. It was a sacred dance on Delos and was said to have been first performed by Theseus as a kind of mime of how he found his way out of the Labyrinth.

The tsamikos, on the other hand, is not a Peloponnesian dance at all: it originated in Roumeli, in Central Greece, and it is an exclusively male dance in which the participants find an opportunity to display their bravery and manliness.

There are plenty of excuses for song and dance in the Peloponnese, with holidays and feast-days occurring regularly everywhere. Easter and the feast of the Virgin (15 August) are the most important, but local saints are celebrated and there are events to mark the anniversaries of victories during the War of Independence.

These feasts may begin as religious observances, but they always end with a banquet - an opportunity to enjoy the cuisine of the Peloponnese. There will be black olives (cured in salt or vinegar) on the table, resinated white or sparkling red wine, and cheese, which in the Peloponnese is usually hard and spicy.

These starters will be followed by pies of all kinds, often with vegetables and even with snails. Meat is usually served roast. Whole lambs will be spit-roasted after the carcase has been rubbed with olive oil and sprinkled with oregano. Suckling goat and pig are usually cooked in the same way. Only hares are boiled, and game birds are very rarely eaten at all. In some places, especially the Mani, pork is pickled and tasty sausages are made with it. Fish fresh from the sea are also a great favourite. Pasta —in its

Greek forms of 'trachanas' and 'hilopittes'— is still made at home, and the women often join forces to make enough for every household.

Fruit is among the dietary staples of the Peloponnese, with water-melons, melons and grapes being the favourite kinds. The women make excellent preserves with cherries, citrus fruit and quinces, as well as pastry cakes filled with walnuts and honey, kourabiedes (dry cakes sprinkled with caster sugar), kataifi (layers of walnut-filled pastry soaked in syrup) and many other appetising delicacies.

Among the attractions of local festivals is that they often afford an opportunity to admire the local traditional dress. Dance companies, in particular, nearly always wear the traditional costume.

The basic element in all the female costumes of the Peloponnese is the blouse. This is usually white and it is embroidered with white or coloured thread around the hem, down the sleeves and at the throat - the parts of it which are visible, that is, since it is almost always worn beneath another garment.

The apron which covers the skirt is there for ornamental purposes only, since it has no practical use. It will be of richly-embroidered silk, or perhaps of wool, with cross-stitched embroidery in multi-coloured cotton thread.

Over the blouse is worn the waistcoat, which is sometimes long and sleeveless, the 'segouna', and sometimes short, tight-fitting at the waist or a little further down, and has long sleeves. On their heads, the women wear kerchiefs; these may be with patterns of flowers —the 'tsemberi'— or white and delicately woven, with gold embroidery and gilded lace round the edges. In Tsakonia the women wear fezzes with long tassels.

The male costume is usually the 'foustanella', the short kilt over leggings worn all over Greece. It is normally worn with a white shirt. The jacket will be either the short cape woven from local wool up in the mountain villages, or a sleeveless waistcoat ('meindani'), or a tight waistcoat with peculiar long sleeves which hand down the back, unbuttoned. The waistcoat is often embroidered in gold. Along the coast of the southern Peloponnese (in the Mani, for example), the men do not wear the foustanella but baggy breeches. On the head, a fez is worn, with a tassel and with a knot of gold wire, rather like a lock of hair. All these costumes are accompanied by gold or silver coins, buckles and chains, while the women often wear jewellery on their foreheads.

Local costumes of the Peloponnese (lithograph, 1816).

A scene from the Patra Carnival, which was first held in 1829.

These costumes can be seen being worn by the dancers at local festivals, some of which include complete theatrical performances. Among such performances is the 'Trial of Barabbas', held on Good Friday each year at Psila Alonia, in Patra, after the Epitafios (the flower-adorned bier of Christ) has been carried round the town, or 'Koutroulis' Wedding' on 'Clean Monday' (the beginning of Lent) at Methoni, where both the 'bride' and the 'groom' are men.

All over the Peloponnese these ancient customs are honoured and respected, and new events are added each year. There are festivals connected with wine and the cultivation of the grape or with the Carnival (Patra leads Greece in this respect), and there are cultural events and festivals with inter-national recognition. Visitors who wish to gain a deeper knowledge of the Peloponnese will find much of its soul in these festivals. And for those whose interest lies principally in the customs of the past, there are numerous folklore museums to give a glimpse of yesteryear.

A tour of the Peloponnese is like an open encyclopaedia, which has much to tell the visitor about its own history and the history of Greece as a whole. Nature adds the dimension of beauty, and the local people will demonstrate in practive that tourism in the land of Zeus Xenios, the god of hospitality, can fill each and every visitor with a wealth of impressions and new experiences. Get ready to go, then; the Peloponnese, stretched out like a mulberry leaf across the Aegean, is waiting.

A tour of the Peloponnese with 44 itineraries

We begin our tour in the Prefecture of **Corinthia**, with its spas and mineral springs close by wooded mountain peaks, caves and lakes. We describe the archaeological sites of Corinth, Nemea, Sikyon, Isthmia and others. Moving south, we enter the orange groves of the Plain of **Argos**, where golden Mycenae awaits us. We also visit Tiryns, historic Argos and the beautiful town of Nafplio. Nearby are the long and cosmopolitan beaches of the Argolic Gulf, and the unique ancient theatre at Epidaurus. **Arkadia** lies in the heart of the Peloponnese, and has fine beaches, archaeological sites on its central plateau and the natural beauties of the Arcadian mountains celebrated in myth. **Achaia** boasts the bustling city of Patra, "capital" of the Peloponnese and the gateway to western Greece. Here, the mountains draw together to form deep gorges, with monasteries on their flanks and spas at their feet. Next to the historic river Alpheios in **Ilia** is Olympia, with its immortal spirit, and higher up is Vases, with its superb temple to Apollo. Further south again is verdant, peaceful **Messinia**, where the Mycenean palace of wise King Nestor can be visited. And our tour ends in **Lakonia**, where fresh suprises are in store in Sparta, with its nearby medieval towns, and in the unique district of the Mani, with its superb caves.

39

ROUTES

The numbering on the map corresponds to the 44 routes of which this guide-book consists. The pages on which each route can be found are as follows:

KORINTHIA 42
 1 Loutraki 45
 2 Korinth - Ancient Korinth 48
 3 Lechaion - Kiato 53
 4 Xylokastro - Stymphalia 55
 5 Korinth - Nemea 58

ARGOLID 60
 6 Ancient Mycenae 64
 7 Argos 69
 8 Argos - Nafplio 70
 9 Nafplio-Tolo-Iria 76
10 Nafplio - Epidaurus 78
11 Epidaurus - Kranidi - Methana 82
12 Argos - Tripoli 85

ARCADIA 86
13 Astros - Leonidi 90
14 Tripoli - Tegea 94
15 Tripoli - Megalopoli 98
16 Megalopoli - A. Karyes 101
17 Megalopoli - Dyrrachi 102
18 Megalopoli - Karytaina 104
19 Tripoli - Astros 106
20 Tripoli - Dimitsana 107
21 Tripoli - Vytina 111
22 Vytina - Langadia 114
23 The Ladonas Dam 115

ACHAÏA 116
24 Diakofto - Kalavryta 119
25 Kalavryta - Tripoli 126
26 Kalavryta - Patra 126
27 Diakofto - Aiyion - Patra 127
   Patra 131
28 Patra - Pyrgos 134
29 Patra - Elia 135

ELIA 136
30 Patra - Gastouni 139
31 Amaliada - Pyrgos 143
32 Ancient Olympia 146
33 Pyrgos - Andritsaina 154
34 Loutra Kaïafa - Messinia 158

MESSINIA 160
35 Kyparissia 163
36 Kyparissia - Pylos 164
37 Pylos - Methoni - Koroni 170
38 Koroni - Ancient Messene 174
   Kalamata 177
39 Kalamata - Kardamyli 180
40 Kalamata - Sparta 183

LACONIA 185
Sparta 187
Mystras 191
41 Sparta - Yeraki 196
42 Sparta - Tripoli 197
43 Sparta - Monemvasia 198
44 Mani 205

SCALE: 1:500.000

KORINTHIA

All the roads from Attica into the Peloponnese cross the Isthmus of Corinth.

The Prefecture of Corinthia is small both in size (2,290 square kilometres) and in population (123,000). Next to the Gulf of Corinth, Greece's largest, the landscape is mild and attractive; along the shores of the Gulf, from Corinth all the way to Patra, are the most fertile parts of the Prefecture. As we move south into the hinterland of the Prefecture, the landscape becomes wilder, and there are imposing peaks and fir-covered mountainsides. Lake Stymphalia, famous from the myths, is another element in this variety of scenery. The climate in its vicinity tends to be much colder.

Once across the Isthmus, one comes to **Corinth** almost immediately. The richest and most populous commercial city of ancient Greece developed on a site of tremendous strategic importance. In order to demonstrate this significance, the ancient Greeks used to say, *"Οὐ παντός πλεῖν ἐς Κόρινθον"* —that is, 'not everyone can travel to Corinth'.

The city was founded by the legendary Sisyphus, a wily monarch who was condemned by the gods to spend eternity rolling a large boulder up a mountain in the underworld. As soon as he got to the top, the boulder rolled back to the bottom and Sisyphus had to start all over again; Sisyphus's fate has made his name a byword for fruitless endeavour.

Despite the alleged fate of its founder, the city and its surrounding area prospered. There were important dynasties of kings, notably the Bacchiads and the Cypselids. It was still prosperous in Roman times.

Although the first thing the Romans did was to raze Corinth, Julius Caesar rebuilt it in 44 BC. Later, it became the most important centre of Christianity in Greece.

Between then and modern times, Corinth passed through the hands of many masters: Goths, Franks, the Azzioli of Florence, the knights of St John (then based in Rhodes), the Palaiologoi, the Turks. Although much of its history was identical with that of the rest of the Peloponnese, there were elements which set it apart and made it known outside Greece. The first of these was the Corinthian Order, the last of the Greek architectural orders, which stood out in par-

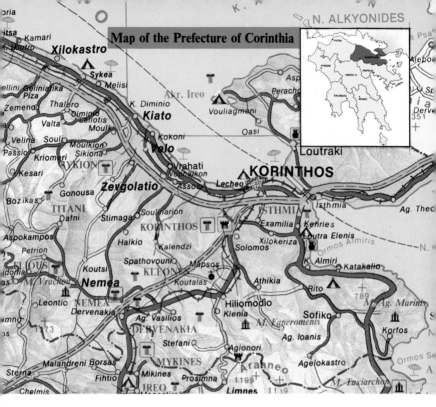

ticular for its complex and richly decorated column capital. Then there was Corinthian pottery, made using yellowish-brown argillaceaous soils or reddish clay. Such pottery was loaded on the ships in Corinth harbour for sale in every corner of the Mediterranean — and still further afield.

The scenes painted on this pottery often depicted myths connected with Corinthia. Heracles, son of Zeus and Alcmene, the most famous, bravest and most glorous hero of the Greek myths, occupied an outstanding place. According to the myth, he came to the Peloponnese equipped with club, bow and arrows, and entered the service of Eurystheus, king of Mycenae. His name went down in history for his twelve feats, at least half of which

were accomplished here in the Peloponnese. Two of them were located in Corinthia: the first of these involved the Harpies of Lake Stymphalia, enormous flesh-eating birds which terrorised the local people, laying waste their fields and carrying off men and women to eat. Heracles killed some of them with his arrows, and scared the rest away. His second feat in this area was to kill the Lion of Nemea, which lived in a cave on Mt Tretus, now known as Korakovouni. Nemea was the site of Panhellenic Games in honour of Zeus Nemeus; in the second and fourth years between each Olympiad there were horse races, running events and musical contests. The victors were awarded wreaths of fresh celery.

mercial assessor wrote of them in the following warm terms:

"To begin with they are green; then they turn reddish-gold, and towards ripeness they are reddish-black. The taste is sweet and very pleasant, like that of Muscat grapes, when they are dried or very ripe; but when they are fresh the taste is delicate and pleasantly sharp. Since it has fewer pips and more juice than more grapes, this variety is a favourite with gourmets, who eat the fruit whole and crack the pips with their teeth" (Felix Beaucour, *Table of Greek Commerce under Turkish Rule, 1787-1797).*

Currants, together with other farming and stock-breeding products, fishing, a limited amount of industry and craft industry, and, of course, tourism, ensure the inhabitants of Corinthia today of a comfortable standard of living. Resorts such as Loutraki, which has for many years been a favourite bathing-place among Athenians, are still busy today. All down the eastern coastline there are countless little bays, with dense vegetation and pretty villages above the waterline where the azure waves lap. Those who prefer inland areas and take to the mountains will find surprises of a different sortin store. To the east of Nemea, on the borders of the Prefecture of Argolida, one of the most important pages in modern Greek history was written. The mountains around the narrow pass of Dervenaki still hold something of the echo of the guns and the clash of swords, for it was here that, during the War of Independence, Kolokotronis and a small force of Greeks ambushed and decimated the much larger troop of Turks under Dramalis. The battle was one of the most important in the War and made a major contribution to Greece's eventual freedom.

Vititors to Nemea in August will no longer find Heracles there, but they will find a wine festival going on. Good wine can, of course, be drunk in Nemea all the year round. Together with olive oil and citrus fruit (oranges and lemons) it is one of Corinthia's principal products. *It is the fruit of the Corinthian vine, which produces excellent wine grapes but, above all, the Corinthian currants which are unique worldwide.* Fresh or dried, currants from Corinth have been sought-after since antiquity. Driving through the villages at the right time of year, the multistoreyed drying racks are everywhere to be seen, bedecked with black currants shrivelling in the sun. Even in early modern times, the grapes of Corinth were appreciated by foreigners as well as by Greeks. An 18th century com-

Loutraki: the seafront of this popular resort.

The temple of Hera at Perachora.

1. Loutraki

The road, just before the bridge over the Corinth Canal forks to the north west, leading, in 6 kms, to **Loutraki**, a pleasant town which combines mountain and seaside scenery.

Its thermal springs have been known since antiquity, and are recommended for a wide variety of different ailments: baths for urinary disorders, arthritis and uric arthritis, together with waters to be taken in cases of gravel, gallstones and dyspepsia. There are also clean beaches, and much to be seen in the surrounding countryside.

Loutraki is one of the longest-established resorts in Greece.

To the north west of Loutraki is **Perachora** (the ancient Peraia Chora), a village with a museum (with a large number of finds from the Heraion of Vouliagmeni); it is famous for its wine.

The road which leaves Perachora to the west takes us, after a pleasant drive of 8 kms, to **Vouliagmeni** (Heraion Lake). The lake has been joined up to the Gulf of Corinth by a short canal, and the tide changes every six hours. There are fine beaches.

Cape Heraion stands a further three kilometres to the west, and a marvellous temple to Hera used to crown it.

Nearly everyone travelling to the Peloponnese will stop for a while at its gates, the Isthmus, at the cafés just beyond the canal, from near which good views of the Canal itself and its two bridges (one road, one rail) may be had.

The Canal was built between 1882 and 1893. Thus, the isthmus of Corinth became a canal and the Peloponnese an island.

Periander, tyrant of Corinth, first had the idea of building a canal, in the 6th century BC. The technical difficulties of such an undertaking, however, forced him to find another solution — the Diolkos, a paved road across the Isthmus which ran from Kalamaki (the ancient Sehoinous) to Poseidonia on the Gulf of Corinth. Ships were dragged across from the bay of Cenchreae to the Gulf of Corinth along this road on carts pulled by people or animals, and then relaunched to continue their journey.

After the road bridge, a fork to the left leads to the ancient site of **Isthmia**, now known as **Kyra Vrysi** (4 kms). Excavations have revealed a temple to Poseidon, the Palaimonion, a theatre, the starting-blocks in the 4th century stadium, where the famous Pan-Hellenic Isthmian games took place, and some remains of the Diolkos. A little ferry links Isthmia with Kalamaki on the opposite shore. Since June 1987 a submersible bridge has been in position on the same site, facilitating chiefly the traffic to and from Epidaurus.

2. Corinth - Ancieht Corinth
   (6 kms)

The main road leads, 5 km from the Isthmus, to **Corinth**. The town, which stands at the head of the Gulf of Corinth, was built in its present situation after disastrous earthquakes in 1858 and 1928.

The town today has an impressive cathedral, dedicated to its patron, St Paul, who taught Christianity and founded one of the most important churches in Greece in Corinth, neo-Classical and modern buildings, and stands in a beautiful setting of sea and mountains.

Four kms to the south is **Examillia**, which takes its name from the 'six-mile walls', a defensive structure on which work began at the time of the Persian Wars. It is worth noting that these were destroyed, rebuilt and supplemented for a full 17 centuries. Further south and to the east, the road brings us to **Kechries**, (the ancient Cenchreae) on the Saronic side, which in ancient times was Corinth's second port (known as Dysca). On the way, the ancient quarries and a large beehive (tholos) tomb may be seen.

Another road, turning to the south of Examillia, runs past the ruins of the Roman aqueduct, through the village of **Xylokeriza**, and finally through a fine landscape of pine and olive groves, running down to little bays, a little to the South of Kechries. At the seaside village of **Almyri** there is a hot sea spring, and **Loutra Oraias Elenis** has sulphur springs (for rheumatism and arthritis). A minor

An aerial photograph of Corinth, with Ancient Corinth in the background, to the right.

Ancient Corinth: the teEple of Apollo, with the Acrocorinth in the background.

road leads further to the south to the pretty villages of Ryto and Sophiko, while the main coast road from the Isthmus via Kechries and Loutra Oraias Elenis carries on to Epidaurus.

Returning to the north side of Corinth, on the road to Patra, the other port of Ancient Corinth, **Lechaion**, lies about 4 km. outside the town. It is unique for the skill with which it was constructed, and there was also a temple to Poseidon in the area (along with the palace of Periander, where the Symposium of the Seven Sages of antiquity was held). There are also the ruins of an impressive Early Christian basilica.

There are roads to the ruins of **Ancient Corinth** from both Corinth itself and Lechaion. The bus takes 20 minutes from Corinth. The city was among the richest and most important in Ancient Greece.

Among the ruins to be seen are those of the Temple of Apollo (6th century, Doric, with only 7 of its monolithic columns —a rare phenomenon in ancient times— still standing), the Agora, the Fountain of Peirene, which has arches and underground channels, the 'sacred spring', with triglyphs, the Bema, or dais, from which the Apostle Paul preached to the Corinthians, various shops, the Fountain of Glauke, the Roman Odeion, the ancient theatre, etc.

A museum operates inside the archaeological site, with fascinating finds from the Agora and prehistoric settlements in the area (Geometric pottery, outstanding examples of Early and Late Corinthian ceramics

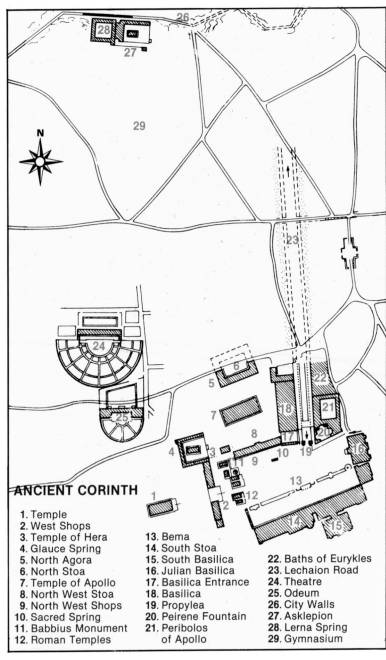

ANCIENT CORINTH

1. Temple
2. West Shops
3. Temple of Hera
4. Glauce Spring
5. North Agora
6. North Stoa
7. Temple of Apollo
8. North West Stoa
9. North West Shops
10. Sacred Spring
11. Babbius Monument
12. Roman Temples
13. Bema
14. South Stoa
15. South Basilica
16. Julian Basilica
17. Basilica Entrance
18. Basilica
19. Propylea
20. Peirene Fountain
21. Peribolos of Apollo
22. Baths of Eurykles
23. Lechaion Road
24. Theatre
25. Odeum
26. City Walls
27. Asklepion
28. Lerna Spring
29. Gymnasium

A Corinthian column capital, and the acanthus plant which inspired it.

with compositions in minute detail, jewellery, bronze weapons and tools, the sacrophagus of a child, a perirhanterion (stoup) from the temple of Poseidon at Isthmia, stone beds, mosaics, Roman murals and statues, Byzantine pottery, etc.

There is also a tourist pavilion on the east side of the ancient theatre. At the entrance to the museum stands a fine example of a Corinthian capital.

The road twists up from the archaeological site to the first gate of the **Acrocorinth** citadel. A tourist pavilion stands in front of the gate.

The Acrocorinth has been fortified since prehistoric times, and at its peak (575 m.) traces have been found of the famous temple of Aphrodite.

The Roman Peirene fountain in Ancient Corinth.

The view over the surrounding countryside is unforgettable. Entering the fort, the visitor will notice traces of masonry from all periods, from ancient times to the previous century.

3. Lechaion - Kiato (17 kms)

The rich plain of Vocha starts at the Lechaion, alongside the Corinth-Patra road, and runs along, full of fruit trees, flowers and vineyards, to the ruins of ancient Sikyon. The old National Road (non toll-paying) runs parallel to the new one, and affords visits to the charming villages of the area.

Kiato stands at about the 21st kilometre. A modern town with ample facilities, it is a centre for the production and processing of cirrants, citrus fruits, tomatoes and other agricultural products, but can also be used as a base for excursions into the fascinating hinterland.

About 6 kms south from Kiato, near the village of **Vasiliko**, lie the ruins of **Sikyon**, one of the most famous cities in the ancient Greek worls.

Sikyon, a member of the Dorian Hexapolis, flourished in all respects under the tyrant Cleisthenes (6th century) and the politician Aratos (3rd century).

Ruins may be seen of the walls, the theatre, two gymnasia, the bouleuterion, the 'sacred spring', the Temple of Artemis, etc. There is a museum in a reconstructed Roman building, with sculpture from the ancient and Hellenistic-Roman periods, pottery from a variety of eras, a 4th century mosaic, and so on.

South west of Kiato, the road to Nea Stymphalia, after the village of

An aerial photograph of Ancient Sikyon; the theatre can be seen on the right.

Souli, forks, leading southwards to many quiet villages: **Paradisi, Kryoneri, Gonousa, Titani, Bozika, Kastraki, Asprokambos, Souli, Ano Pasio, Trikala, Psari, Kaliani, Skoteini** and **Galatas**.

Continuing to the south west, the road to **Nea Stymphalia** (Driza) passes through the village of **Kionia** (with springs and abundant trees), before coming, higher up, to the lake, in a thickly vegetated area. The ruins of ancient **Stymphalos** (walls, altars, springs, a stadium, etc.) lie on the west bank.

It was here that ancient mythology located the home of the 'Stymphalian birds' and the labour of Hercules by which he dealt with them. Near the road are the ruins of a temple of Artemis and the 13th century Frankish church of Zaraka.

Hadrian's aqueduct, one of the finest construction projects of antiquity, which starts from the east side of the lake, gave water to Corinth and is still used for irrigation in the plain.

Side roads run off up the sides of Mt Zireia (Kyllini) to particularly attractive villages: **Lafka, Karteri, Kastania** —which has a hotel some 1,300 m. up— **Mati, Panorama, Kalyvia, Mesino** or **Zevgolatio, Mousia, Goura, Steno, Pheneos**.

In a small museum at Kalyvia there is a statue of a woman with inset eyes and eyelashes. Near the village is the Monastery of St George 'Phonias', with a hostel. The monastery was fortified by Kolokotronis when attacked by Ibrahim.

There are remains of a Frankish castle at **Tarsos**, near Goura. Underground channels leading from the drained lake of Pheneos allow rain-water to drain away.

Continuing along the coast road from Kiato towards Patra, we pass through **Neapolis** (with a by-road to **Pasio** and **Megalos Valtos**), and then **Diminio**. The scenery is very pretty. A road from **Ano Diminio** leads up the sides of Mt Zireia, through the thickly-wooded villages of **Lalioti, Megalos Valtos** and **Mikros Valtos** before reaching the village of **Throfari**, 670 m. up.

At approximately 29 kms from Corinth along the coast, just outside the village of **Melissi**, a Mycenean grave may be seen. A little further on, as we enter the village of **Tholero**, stands a pine tree under which the poet Angelos Sikelianos wrote many of his works.

Sykia, 3 kms from Melissi, is the starting-point for an idyllic stretch of verdand coastline, leonwn as **Pefkias**. There are tourist amenities, and the beach runs as far as Xylokastro, 2 km away.

The Pefkias beach at Xylokastro.

4. Xylokastro - Stymfalia
(43 kms)

Xylokastro, has been called the Côte d'Azur of Greece. It attracts visitors all the year round, drawn by its combination of sea and mountain charms, its pine trees, flowers and orchards.

It was first settled after the 1821 Revolution by Greeks from Trikala and the Pheneos plain, although it is mentioned during the Turkish period as a port. It has modern tourist facilities, where large numbers of Greek and foreign visitors stay each year.

An attractive road leads from Xylokastro to **Stylia** (Vlandousia), **Panariti, Markasi** (Manna) and **Zemeno** (which produces excellent wine).

Just outside Xylokastro is a side road to the chapel of St Yerasimos, who is the patron saint of Cephallonia. The church was built in 1622, in a lovely situation, and, apart from a hostel, has a fine collection of Byzantine treasures, including icons, manuscripts, lamps, candelabra, wood carvings, crucifixes, etc. St Yerasimos himself was descended from the famous Byzantine Notaras family from the nearby village of Trikala.

A charming and varied route leads from just outside Xylokastro to **Riza, Dendro, Rethi** and **Trikala**.
Trikala, which has facilities for tourists, is the starting-point for climbers wishing to ascend Mt Zireia. It takes two hours on foot to reach **Lake Dasiou**, surrounded by firs and

The mythical lake of Stymphalia, on the banks of which Ancient Stympalos stoo

willows, and another two from there to the highest peak of Zireia (2,400 m.). From the top, climbers enjoy an extensive view over the fine **Zarouchla** forest and across to the imposing bulk of **Mt Helmos** (Aroania). The

also ski slopes, which are usable from about Christmas to the beginning of April. A small ski-tow operates.

Half an hour from the shelters (to the East) lies one of the most impressive caves in Greece, the **Cave of Hermes**, which has marvellous stalactites.

The coast road from Xylokastro to Patra leads on through **Kamari** (with abundant trees and vineyards), **Kato Loutro, Kato Pitsa, Lykoporia, Stomio** —where there is a by-road to **Byzianika** and **Pyrgo**— **Lygia, Vodia**, and finally **Derveni**.

The road is memorable for its fine sea and mountain views. Derveni is well-known as a tourist centre, with amenities, and can also be used as a base for trips into the surrounding area.

Just after Derveni a road leads south to **Evrostina**, at a height of 550 m. which has groves of cherry and apple trees, and, further up, at **Sopoto**, to the chapel of Ayia Eleousa (900 m.), an ideal spot for camping with a plentiful water supply, and the **Evrostina** plateau, at 1,000 m. with fine views down to the plain and the Gulf of Corinth and across to the mountains of Central Greece. The road then goes on to **Karya** and **Sarantapicho** (1,000 m.), near which there is accommodation at 1,300 m. with a cave from which a panoramic view of the villages around Kalavryta may be had.

Still further to the South, beyond the village of **Tarsos**, we come to the archaeological site of Pheneos, and the striking of the village of Kastania, before returning to the mythical Lake Stymphalia (see p. 54).

re Heracles performed one of his 12 feats.

two mountain shelters on Zireia lie two and a half and three hours, respectively, from Trikala. There are

Ancient Nemea: the ruins of the famous temple of Zeus.

5. Corinth - Nemea
(36 kms)

South of Corinth there are two roads which may be taken to Tripoli, at the heart of the Peloponnese. The old road, 110 kms long, which passes through Argos, has much of interest along the route and runs along the Argolic Gulf before climbing to the inhospitable Achladokampos plain. This road is the one to be chosen for an exploration of the region. The new road cuts 30 kms off the distance and halves the time taken. It passes through mountainous country and has little to offer the sightseer; it is, however, a way of reaching Tripoli quickly, and from there one can either go south or into the surrounding countryside (p. 95).

Hiliomodi lies 18 kms from Corinth; from there a fork of the old road leads to **Klenia** (built on the site of the ancient city of Tenea), where, among other things, the famous Kouros of Tenea was found. One of the most perfect of ancient statues, it can be seen in the Munich Glyptotek.

The old road continues westwards from Hiliomodi. At approximately 25 kms from Corinth it comes to ancient Kleonai, which played an important role in Peloponnesian history from Mycenean times to the 2nd century B.C. The American Archaeological School has discovered traces of a Bronze Age settlement at Zygouries.

At a point 31 kms along the road, there is a branch off to the north west, with **Irakleio** 4 kms along this; this is the site of **Ancient Nemea**, another important city. It was famous in ancient times for its Panhellenic Games (the 'Nemea'), which featured contests in gymnastics, horse-riding, music and drama.

According to tradition, Nemea was founded by Heracles after he had killed the Lion of Nemea, but it is also held that the city was established by the seven generals of Argos ('Seven against Thebes') in honour of Opheltes or Archemorus, son of King Lycurgus of Nemea. The Games were conducted inside the precincts of the Temple of Zeus, ruins of which have been discovered near the entrance into Irakleio, about 200 m. from the road. The temple, which was a Doric peripteron, is said to have been built in the 4th century according to plans by the sculptor Scopas. Traces of a gymnasium of the Classical period have also been found, with a palaestra and Roman baths to the South.

American archaeologists have discovered, among other things, the whole of the Temple of Zeus, as well as the stadium where the games were held every two years (from 573 BC onwards). The work of reconstructing the Temple of Zeus from the fragments scattered about the site has already begun. To the west of the village is the hill-top of Tsoungiza where the American School found the prehistoric settlement mentioned above. To the east of Irakleio, on the slopes of Mt Tritos, is a cave with two entrances, which tradition says was the lair of the Nemean Lion, killed by the hero and demi-god Heracles in the course of his Labours. A rather strange variation on the myth is that the lion originally resided on the Moon, from which it was hurled down to the Earth.

A road leads West through Koutsomodi to **Nemea** (the modern village, famed for its wine), to the north west of which is a fertile plain full of vineyards. The idyllic nature of the countryside is supplemented by olive groves clambering up the surrounding slopes.

Two interesting trips can be made from Nemea. The first (3 km) is to the monastery and Byzantine church of Our Lady of the Rock, to the south, where a hostel operates.

If we continue south on the central road, at 31 kms on the Corinth-Argos road, at the turning for Ancient Nemea and Nemea, we enter the pass of **Dervenakia**, where, in July 1822, the Greeks, under Kolokotronis, ambushed and routed the Turkish army of Dramali in one of the most decisive battles in the War of Independence.

A little earlier (at kilometre 29) a side road to the south leads to the rise of Ayios Sostis, where a statue of Kolokotronis has been erected.

After some bends, we pass **Chani Anesti**, where two tavernas among the plane trees invite the traveller to rest a while. A little further along is the border between Corinthia and the Argolid.

ARGOLID

"The traveller who crosses the eastern Morea in the direction of its southern tip will through the gloomy defiles and across the mountainsides of Nemea and then, soon after, will see a huge and fertile plain open up before him. Under the wide-bosomed vault of the sky, which shortly before had censed him in the wilderness with the aroma of thyme, Nature now stretches out in lighter-hearted vein. This is a quiet place, with thick, well-aerated soil, whose flesh is succulent, which lies there year by year, given over entirely to the mystic ritual of regeneration. This blessed land is the plain of the Argolid".

(Angelos Terzakis, *Princess Isambo*).

The promontory of the Argolid, rather like an island, really is a blessed place, with its mild winters and warm, dry summers. The mountains which stand above its 2,145 square kilometres are low: Arachnaio, Trapezounda, Oneia. It has rivers with ancient names —Erasinos, Inachos and the seasonal torrent of the Xerias— to water its earth, one of whose best-known products is the fragrant melon.

Whever one looks in the Argolid, there is evidence that the course of history has never been interrupted. Argos, the capital of the Prefecture, stands on exactly the same site as the ancient city Argos. And if some of the other towns became famous in later times, that was merely because they had to wait their turn in patience. Nafplio is an example of this: although its history stretches back 3,000 years, it was not until the Middle Ages, under Venetian rule, that its fame began to spread. Nafplio was one of the first capitals of newly-liberated Greece.

Map of the Prefecture of Argolida

A huge Venetian castle stands above the town, keeping unsleeping watch over it and the surrounding plain. This is the Palamidi, reached by 999 steps from the centre of the town. From its battlements, there is a superb view of the little fortress of Bourtzi, lying in the bay.

Here the visitor can stroll through the narrow lanes with their two and three-storeyed neo-Classical houses, or walk along the seafront, or visit the town's monuments and museums, where memories of the recent or the distant past are waiting, or simply enjoy the sense of timeless nobility and gentleness which Nafplio emits. All these features make it one of Greece's most attractive towns, and it greets many thousands of visitors each year.

The coastline to the east and south of Nafplio is a long green and azure strip of spas, resorts and cosmopolitan holiday centres running all the way to the eastern extremity of the Peloponnese.

To the south-west of Nafplio we pass through the area known as 'Achladokampos'. Although its name, strictly speaking, means 'plain of the pear trees', it is said that when Kolokotronis was passing through during the War of Independence, he was struck by the number of olive trees: *"Ach! Ladokampos"* ('plain of olive oil') he cried, and the name stuck.

Olives, cereals, and fruit of all possible kinds are the basic crops around which the occupations of the Prefecture's 93,000 inhabitants revolve. However, the tourist trade is growing too, and employing more and more local people to provide services for the thousands of visitors who flock to see the sights of the Argolid.

This "blessed land" was celebrated in verse by Homer, Aeschylus, Sophocles and Euripides. Even today,

on the cool summer evenings in Epidaurus, the ancient invocation, *"ἰώ Κυκλωπίς ἑστία· ἰώ πατρίς, Μυκίνα φίλα"* ('Oh, strong-built corner of my home, oh, my native land, oh, my beloved Mycenae') can still be heard. The ancient sense of measure and rhythm live on in Epidaurus today, at the annual Festival of Ancient Drama, where the ancient progress through time and human existence can be seen to reach its close, forming a perfect circle.

The history of this Prefecture is most important. Human occupation here dates back to the Mesolithic epoch, and perhaps even earlier, and the first sites where man dwelt were at Ermionida, Argos and Tirnys. This was where the great civilisation of Mycenae flourished, and this was the home of the Atreides, the powerful dynasty which led Greece into the ten years of the Trojan War. Here lived kings, queens and princes who were all too subject to the common passions. While the Classical period in Greece stood out for its search for moderation and rhythm, one has to think, as one visits Tiryns, Mycenae or Asine that the people who built those cities were trying to transcend their own measure, their own limitations. Their 'Cyclopean' walls, nearly two metres thick, were such imposing structures that the generations which came after them could only conclude that the Cyclopes, a mythical race of supermen, had built them. They buried their famous dead in huge tholos tombs, accompanied by priceless gold artefacts. What we see today are the remnants of a civilisation which sought to break free of the bounds of the known world — and succeeded in doing so. The power of Mycenae spread across the seas from Cyprus to the coast of Asia Minor, to the land of the Phoenicians, to Africa and to the Pharaohs of Egypt.

6. Ancieht Mycenae

At the village of **Fichtia**, 41 kms along the old Corinth-Argos-Tripoli road (see p. 58), there is a fork to the east which leads to Mycenae.

The ruins of the ancient city stand on a rocky knoll. The site commands all the ancient roads to neighbouring and more distant cities.

Findings to date reveal that Mycenae was first inhabited before 2000 BC. Legend has it that Mycenae was founded by the hero Perseus, son of Zeus and Danae, who was the daughter of King Acrisius of Argos. On his return from a long and enforced sojourn in Asia, Perseus brought the Cyclops with him, and they built the city's massive walls.

Mycenae reached its peak after 1600 BC. When the Minoan civilisation fell, their place was taken by Mycenae, which built a commercial and military empire stretching over all the Eastern Mediterranean. Mycenean dominance lasted until the 11th century BC.

The first dynasty of rulers ended with Eurystheus (grandson of Perseus and cousin of Heracles, whom he required to carry out the twelve labours). The Pelopid (Atreid) dynasty followed, and at this time Mycenae reached its zenith. The tragic Atreids —and especially Agamemnon— have inspired poets and dramatists ever since.

Archaeologists have discovered the acropolis, various tombs on and around it, and the ruins of houses and other buildings within the city. The Lion Gate, which stands at the entrance to the acropolis, and shows

Mycenae: the Lion Gate.

two —now headless— lionesses, is world-famous.

The lionesses form part of an enormous triangular block, which rests on the equally massive lintel stone. Between them is a symbolic column. Inside the acropolis, the royal burying-ground has been excavated, revealing six royal shaft graves set in a double circle and contained by a wall. The tombs, which were of kings and their families, contained gold, silver, copper, bronze and pottery, jewellery, household equipment, weapons and other objects.

Most of these may be seen in the Archaeological Museum in Athens. The ruins of other buildings, including houses and a temple area,

THE ARCHAEOLOGICAL SITE OF MYCENAE

1. The House of Sphinxes
2. The House of the Oil Merchant
3. The House of the Seashells
4. The West House
5. Grave Circle B
6. The 'Tomb of Clytemnestra'
7. The 'Tomb of Aegisthus'
8. The Spring of Perseus
9. The Prehistoric Cemetery
10. The Lion Gate
11. The Granary
12. Grave Circle A
13. Ramp
14. The House of the Ramp
15. **16, 17, 18 Houses**
19. The Palace
20. Foundations of temple dating from the historical period
21. The House of the Columns
22. North Postern Gate
23. Secret, Cistern, Underground Passage
24. Sally Port

N

have also been found in the acropolis. The walls are from 3 to 7 metres thick and as much as 14 metres on the north side, where they contained a secret exit and tunnels leading to a hiding-place and a water tank outside the walls.

The large beehive tombs outside the walls are also impressive, while a second grave circle (that inside the acropolis is regarded as the first) yielded another 25 untouched tombs with valuable grave offerings.

The entrance to the 'Treasury of Atreus'.

The acropolis of Mycenae dominates the fertile plain of the Argolid.

Ruins of other buildings, including a Hellenistic theatre and houses, have also been found in the area round the acropolis. Three of the beehive tombs have been imaginatively named the Treasury of Atreus (or Tomb of Agamemnon), the Tomb of Clytemnestra and the Tomb of Aegisthus. However, these names can hardly be justified, since the three bee-hive tombs, date from a much earlier period.

Inscriptions in Linear B have been found in the lower city.

The wealth and brilliance of the funerary offerings in the royal tombs at Mycenae helped give the city its epithet of 'rich in gold'

Only the most important dead were granted death-masks such as this one; the unknown king of Mycenae to whom it belonged has traditionally been given the name of Agamemnon.

A fresco of a female figure from a house on the Acropolis at Mycenae.

Rings were made with delicate art in semi-precious stones and precious metals and were decorated with religious, hunting and duelling scenes.

These are bronze daggers, inlaid with decorative motifs in gold, silver and niello (a black metallic substance) are the culimination of Mycenean art.

7. Argos

From the village of **Fichtia** the old Corinth-Argos-Tripoli road continues south and at the 50th kilometre reaches **Argos**, commercial centre of the area, built on the site of a part of the ancient city.

The city had periods of great power and economic and artistic influence. Indeed, so great was the city's power and brilliance that Homer and other ancient writers frequently refer to inhabitants of the Peloponnese in general, or even of Greece, as Argives. However, Sparta frequently questioned the right of Argos to dominate the area and there were often wars between the two cities.

Although Argos kept its importance throughout the Roman period, Byzantium and the Turks put an end to its might. The city was, however, important during the War of Independence, both as a strategic centre and as a source of supplies.

Since the last century, the town has developed into a major agricultural, commercial and, more recently, industrial centre.

On the rock Larisa, which towers over the town, there are remains of a Pelasgian citadel with Frankish and Venetian additions and alterations. The acropolis had a temple to Akraian Hera, and there are Byzantine and Venetian ruins.

View of Argos. The castle can be seen and to the rear the Argive Plain.

A nearby hill (Aspida) displays ruins of a Mycenean palace and other buildings of the same period.

To the south west of the city is an archaeological site containing the Agora, the theatre —unique for its seats hewn out of the rock— and a Roman Odeion with a fine mosaic floor.

There is an impressive church to Our Lady of the Rock half way up the Larisa rock. Of the other churches, St Peter's (patron saint — the church is the seat of the local bishop) and St John the Baptist's are of interest — the first National Assembly of the Greeks was held in the courtyard of the latter in 1821.

Two halls of the town museum house finds from excavations at Argos, Lerna and elsewhere, among them a fine three-mouthed amphora, a rare bronze helmet and cuirass, Mycenean pottery, idols and other small objects, an extremely fine collection of a large mosaic showing the months and seasons, etc.

About 7 km to the north west are the ruins of the Argive Heraion, a Doric temple and one of the most famous in the Peloponnese. Important games, the Heraia, were held here in the middle of the period between Olympiads.

8. Argos - Nafplio
(12 kms)

On the Argos-Nafplio road we pass through the village of **Argoliko**, above which rise the imposing ruins of ancient Tiryns, next to the Argos-Nafplio road.

Ancient Tiryns would appear to have been inhabited since about 3000 BC, and its importance can be guessed from the majesty of its acropolis and strength of its walls.

Legend has it that the walls were built by seven Cyclops from Lycia. The walls are made of huge irregular boulders (some of them weighing up to 13 tons) and they are similar to those at Mycenae. Their breadth varies between 8 and 10 metres. The impressive underground areas must have been used as storerooms during times of peace and as shelters for the local population in wartime.

Inside the acropolis, ruins have been discovered of a circular palace of the third millenium, Middle Helladic (2000-1600 BC) walls, an imposing Mycenean palace of the 12th-13th century with fine murals, and other buildings.

In less than four kilometres we come to the outskirts of Nafplio.

Nafplio is very ancient; myths tell us that it was founded by Nauplius, son the sea god Poseidon. There was a famous spring, known as the Spring of Amynone, where the goddess Hera was reputed to wash herself, thus regaining her virginity. Nauplius built the city round the spring, protecting it with Cyclopean walls, parts of which may still be seen today. His son Palamides, who gave his name to the rock looming above the town, led a detachment of Nauplians in the Trojan War.

The imposing corridors of Tiryns.

An aerial photograph of Nafplio.

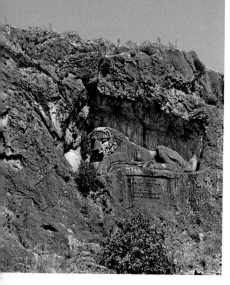

Nafplio impresses the visitor with its singular nobility: it has old houses, courtyards filled with trees and pots of herbs, elegant balconies and charming narrow streets.

Those streets take our thoughts and memories back through history as we see monuments such as the Bavarian monument of a lion carved on the rock by the German sculptor Siegel or the historic Venetian castle of Bourtzi, lying lazily on the waters of the Argolic Gulf. These sights make up a unique image which thousands of visitors enjoy each year from the tables of the pretty cafes and restaurants on the waterfront.

Nafplio is a relaxing stop for every traveller.

Nafplio (Nauplia) was an independent city until 676 BC, when it was conquered and destroyed by Damocrates, King of Argos, who turned it into a port for Argos. Those Nafpliots who escaped took refuge in Methoni.

From then on for more than 1,200 years the town remained in obscurity. The Byzantines mention it in 589 AD as 'Nafplio'. The town was successively occupied by the Franks, Venetians and Turks, but in 1718 it came firmly and finally under Turkish rule. Nafplio rose in revolt at the very beginning of the War of Independence and was surrendered by the Turks on 1 December 1822.

Ioannis Capodistrias, first Governor of Greece, landed at Nafplio on 7 January 1828, and in 1823. Nafplio became the first capital of free Greece until Athens took over the role in 1834. King Otho, first King of free Greece, landed here in January 1833.

The town today is an agricultural, commercial and industrial centre. Among the sights are: the Venetian castle on the Palamidi (with the dungeon where Kolokotronis was imprisoned, and impressive ruins), the Acronafplia cape (medieval ruins, Capodistrias' barracks —later a prison— and modern tourist facilities), the Venetian fort of Bourtzi in the centre of the harbour (now a hotel), and many of the buildings in the town itself.

One might mention the Byzantine-style Church of St George (built in

1619), with murals of the 18th century Italian school, including a copy of Leonardo's 'Last Supper', the first Greek School, which opened in 1832, the Church of St Spyridon, the Catholic Church of the Transfiguration, (an old monastery which later became a mosque), the building where the first Greek Parliament met, Constitution Square, under whose plane tree the leaders of the War of Independence used to meet, with the Pupil-Teacher School of Capodistrias, the Museum and Public Library, Iatron Filellinon and Trion Navarchon Squares, and in the suburb of Pronia, National Academy Square and the Five Brothers, a small fortified outpost with five canons defending the Bourtzi and the Acronafplia.

The Lion of the Bavarians (1840) may be seen carved in the rock on the way to the picturesque suburb of Pronia.

The Archaeological Museum (Constitution Square) contains finds from the major sites in the area, menhirs from Midea, an ancient city on the western slopes of Mt Arachnaion, near the villages of Dendra and Merbaka, a rich collection of pottery, sections of murals and Linear B inscriptions from Mycenae, copper tools, artefacts and weapons, etc.

There is also a Folk Museum (1 Vas. Alexandrou St), set up by the V. Antoniou Peloponnesian Folkore Foundation.

A typical sunset over Nafplio, with all its colours.

9. Nafplio - Tolo - Iria
(26 kms)

The road to Epidaurus leaves Nafplio in an easterly direction and passes through the village of **Aria**.

A branch to the right leads to **Lefkakia** (2 kilometres) and from there, by a branch to the right (south west), to **Asine** and **Ancient Asine**.

Excavations here have brought to light pre-Mycenean buildings as well as a Mycenean graveyard and acropolis, the Cyclopean walls of which are impressive and similar to those of other Mycenean cities.

The head of a Mycenean idol (Asine).

Tolo is a modern seaside res.

About two kilometres from Asine the road ends at **Tolo**, a pretty seaside town with a long fine beach and good swimming. There are abundant hotels, restaurants and camp sites. Two islands can be seen off-shore, and these are rich in partridges.

A road from Lefkakia to the left (south-east) passes through the villages of **Drepano** and **Kantia** before, after a turn to the south, ending at **Iria** and **Iria Beach**, a popular area with tourists for its sandy beach and attractive landscape.

The beach at Asine.

sun-bathing, swimming and sea sports.

10. Nafplio - Epidaurus
(30 kms)

The main road which leaves Nafplio for Epidaurus in an easterly direction passes through the village of **Aria**. Near here stands the Church of Ayia Moni (Zoodochou Pighi), a fine example of Byzantine architecture dating from 1149. The spring which bubbles up from under the shady plane trees is the Canathos Spring (or Spring of Amynone) of antiquity. Ayia Moni is now a nunnery.

Ligourio (25 km from Nafplio) is a large and attractive village among mountains near Epidaurus. There are Byzantine churches, and an ancient inscription found at Ligourio shows the route taken by visitors to the Asklepeion (ancient Epidaurus) in antiquity.

Old Epidaurus
with its little harbour and picturesque shores.

At Ligourio the road forks. The branch to the north brings us in a few kilometres to **Palia Epidaurus**, **Nea Epidaurus**, where the first Greek National Assembly was held in December 1821, the pretty village of **Paralia** and the Agnountos Monastery. The remains of a Frankish castle can be distinguished on the hill overlooking Palia Epidaurus.

The road continues northwards with small branches off to the villages of Dimaina, Sofiko and Angelokastro, entering the Prefecture of Corinthia.

The eastern branch of the main road turns south east to begin with and then north east and soon enters the beautiful wooded Asclepius area and the famous theatre.

Artistic creation is closely linked to the technical perfection of the theater in this sacred area of the Asclepeio.

In ancient times, **Epidaurus** was famous mainly for its Asklepeion, -a sanctuary devoted to the healer-god Asclepius. However, the site was first used as a sacred place of the god Malus, who later became identified with Apollo Maleatas. The sanctuary of Malus was about 2 kilometres away, near what is today the church of St Anne.

In Homeric times, when 'healers' are first encountered, these belonged to the ranks of heroes, generals and kings. Frequently, however, they also carried out the duties of priests. Their medicine was empirical and herbs formed the means of treatment. With Asclepius, medicine was elevated to a divine science, and we can see that the appearance of the first doctor coincides with the domination of medicine by religion.

The fame of Epidaurus as a healing centre was such that it attracted the sick from all over Greece and from other parts of the ancient world. Therapy was based on sleep treatment ('encoemesis') but surgery was also performed. Inscriptions record cases of cures which produce admiration in medical circles even today — the dead were occasionally brought back to life, for example. Asclepius himself has given rise to some dispute, as have his medical talents. He appears to have lived around the 13th century B.C. and to have been deified later, but his origin is unclear. Although most legends say he was the son of Apollo, a local variation has him brought up on Mount Myrtion, whose name was changed to Titthion in honour of a goat which suckled him. Today, the mountain is called Theokafsto.

The best preserved and restored ancient structure at Epidaurus is the theatre, the work of Polycleites the Younger, an architect and sculptor of Argos, who also designed the circular Tholos. The theatre, which seats 14,000, has always been famous for the harmony of its design and the perfection of its acoustics. Ruins of the ancient stadium (5th century BC) may also been seen. Every four years, ten days after the Isthmian Games, athletic and musical contests were held here. We can also see the Temple of Asclepius (4th century, designed by the architect Theodotus and with sculpture by Timotheus), the Abaton, where the sick slept, (or 'encoemeterion') temples to Artemis, Themis, Hygeia and Aphrodite, colonnades and baths, a gymnasium (on which the Romans built an Odeion) and the Katagogion (probably a hostel).

The Museum houses parts of the Tholos and the Asclepius temple, inscriptions on columns recording miraculous cures, a Corinthian capital by Polycleites, decorative pottery and reconstructions of parts of the sacred area, Classical, Hellenistic and Roman sculpture, copper objects, surgical instruments, etc.

An aerial photograph of the archaeological site. The Odeum can be discerned in the foreground, with the ancient 'hostel', the Museum and the Theatre.

Porto Cheli bay: in its waters rests a part of the ancient city of Alieis.

11. Epidaurus - Kranidi - Methana (118 kms)

The branch of the road which turns south east from Ligourio (before Ancient Epidaurus) has a turn to the right (south) which leads to its more southerly section, towards Kranidi.

After the villages of **Adami** and **Trachia**, there is a fork at **Neochori**. To the right (south), the road continues to the crossroads with the minor road which leads to the villages of **Kanapitsa**, **Karnezeïka** and **Iria**. Approximately 7 kms from Karnezeïka is the Monastery of Avgo (dedicated to St Demetrius), perched on the edge of a wild gorge.

Continuing southwards, the road passes through the villages of **Rado**, **Didyma** (on the site of the small ancient city of the same name, with two chasms and curious geological phenomena), **Fourni** and **Kampos**. The branch off to the north west ends in a picturesque little inlet with an island-style fishing village called **Kilada**; it has a tradition of building fishing boats.

From the crossroads, the road continuing south enters the town of **Kranidi**, which has a long-established seafaring tradition.

A road leaves Kranidi to the south west and leads to the very beautiful resort of **Porto Heli**, at the head of a small bay where much tourist development has taken place in recent years and there is a wide range of modern amenities. Porto Heli is built on the site of the ancient city Alieis or Aliki, and an ancient cemetery has been excavated, producing graves and funerary offerings of the Classical period. The ruins of ancient buildings may be discerned on the sea-bed in the harbour. In the Byzantine church of St George there is a signature of Michael Palaeologus.

Passing another bay to the south, the road goes on to another popular resort: that of **Kosta**, with a fine beach and good swimming, which lies opposite the beautiful island of Spetses. The island may be reached by launch — frequent sailings.

Another road, leaving Kranidi to the east, brings us to the idyllic seaside **Ermioni**, set among lemon, orange and olive trees. The village is built on the site of the ancient city of the same name, of which some ruins have been found.

The island of **Dokos**, which lies off Ermioni, was fortified by the Byzantines (ruins of the castle can be seen). Dokos exports valuable coloured marble.

The Nunnery of Ayii Anargyri, a short way to the West from Ermioni, has a bitter spring in its courtyard.

From Ermioni the road continues along the coast and at 42 kms we reach **Galatas**, opposite the beautiful island of Poros (frequent connections by ferry).

There has been tourist development here recently. The vegetation in the surrounding area is lush, and a famous forest of lemon trees stands nearby.

Galatas as seen from Poros.

The road turns north west, along the coast, and soon a turning to the left (south west) reaches **Damalas** (Troezen), where the Third National Assembly met durning the War of Independence. The ruins of **Ancient Troezen**, birthplace of the mythical hero Theseus, lie close by between two ravines.

Ruins have been found of walls, a tower, sanctuaries of Hippolytus and Pan, baths, ancient tombs with funerary inscriptions in relief etc. There are also Byzantine churches. The Devil's Bridge, standing over a deep ravine full of plane trees, stands about 1 km away. The name reflects the popularly reputed creator of the bridge.

Nine kilometres north west of Galatas is **Methana**, a resort with a fine beach at the bottom of green slopes. The town has sulphur springs, supposedly useful in the treatment of rheumatism, arthritis, dermatological complaints and disorders of the nervous system.

The remains of ancient walls of polygonal stones can be seen at the bottom of the harbour. The small peninsula on which Methana stands is volcanic, and the village **Kaimeni** stands on its northwestern extremity, and at the summit of the cone, nearby, from which the crater (no longer active) may be seen. It has a diameter of 150 metres and a depth of 60, and Strabo describes a violent eruption.

Methana, whose medicinal springs were famous as far back as the 3rd century BC.

12. Argos - Tripoli
(57 kms)

From Argos, one branch of the main road runs south west, and after 5 kms a minor road turns to the right (West) to **Kefalari**, a charming wooded spot next to a picturesque chapel of the Zoodochos Piyi built into the rock. The waters rises from the springs of the Erasinos river. In antiquity, there were celebrations here each year in honour of Dionysos and Pan. Nowadays, there is an important feast on the Friday of easter week.

On a hill two kilometres away to the south west are the ruins of a triumphal pyramid built by Argos to mark a victory over Sparta.

At about 10 km from Argos we reach the ruins of **Ancient Lerna**, spread around the village of **Myli**. This is where the hero and demi-god Heracles slew the Hydra, the mythical beast with nine (or, according to which version of the myth one reads, more) heads.

Myli acquired significance during the War of Independence thanks to its strategic position on the road to Tripoli. Theodoros Kolokotronis, leader of the revolutionary forres, had his headquarters here in August 1822, and the Revolutionary Government ran the siege of Nafplio from the spot in 1824.

It was near Myli, in June 1825, that Dimitrios Ipsilantis defeated the army of Ibrahim in a battle during which General Makriyannis was wounded.

The main road continues to the south. After a while, a fork to the right (west) leads on to the twisting mountain road to Achladokampos, in the direction of Tripoli. The smaller road to the left takes us through **Kiveri**, with a fine beach and thence into Kynouria, and on to Astros and Paralia Astrous.

The Achladokampos road has fine views to offer us, as it twists through gorges and glens with the sea opening out beneath us. Another turning to the left (south) also leads along a minor road through some villages to Astros.

Twenty eight kms from Argos we see the mountain village of **Achladokampos**. A hill to the west of the village preserves remains of the small Byzantine town of Mouchli, which had 365 churches. Today only Our Lady 'Mouchliotissa' remains. Traces of a temple to Artemis have come to light on the lower slopes of Mt Artemision, nearby.

As the main road continues, the bends become somewhat fewer, and 34 km from Argos we reach the 'Hani' (Inn) of Thodoros, a favourite spot for a rest and some food. On a low hill next to the Hani can be seen the ruins of the acropolis of ancient Hysiae.

The main road continues uphill towards Mt Parthenion, entering Arcadia and approaching Tripoli.

ARCADIA

In the heart of the Peloponnese lies the fourth-largest Prefecture in Greece. Arkadia stretches over an area of 4,418 square kilometres, with high snowy mountains —Mainalo (1,935m), Parnon (1,935 m), Saita (1,812m), Skiathio (1,800m)— covered in shady forests of pine, fir and chestnut. There are grazing lands and cultivated areas where a variety of crops are grown. Mt Mainalo has an excellent skiing centre, yet not far to the east are the sunny beaches of Kynouria. In Arkadia, nature has been tireless in providing alternation in the landscape. The same is true of the climate: it is mildest along the superb coastline at Astros, near attractive Leonidio, and at Tyros, but it becomes more continental as we move towards the mountainous centre of the Prefecture. There is heavy rain and frequent snow in winter, and Tripoli, the capital of the Prefecture, enjoys the lowest temperatures in the whole of the Peloponnese.

Arcadians: a lithograph of 1816.

Despite all this beauty, the population of Arkadia— and of the upland areas in particular— has been falling constantly in recent years. People have moved out in search of a better life in Athens and abroad. Life is hard in isolated villages in the forests, by the side of rushing torrents, and perhaps the state has not displayed the interest it should have shown. In 1951, Arkadia's population was 154,361; in 1961 it was down to 134,950 and by 1971 to 111,263. The decline has not stopped there, and today Arkadia has no more inhabitants than does Corinthia in half the area. When the inhabitants left, they abandoned their fine two storey stone-built houses; entire villages of superb examples of traditional architecture were in danger of crumbling away. In recent years, however, restoration work has begun, and the state has placed preservation orders on whole villages —such as Stemnitsa— to ensure that their character remains unchanged.

For those who have remained, the coasts provide good fishing, the plain of Megalopolis, watered by the Alpheios, the largest river in the Peloponnese, is suitable for farming, and the mountainsides are still alive with innumerable flocks of sheep and goats. Indeed it was the pastoral life which made Arkadia famous worldwide; in world literature, 'Arcadian' came to signify the kind of rural life that seemed ideal — at least to those who did not have to live it. Many great works of art have taken Arkadia as their theme, including Poussin's famous picture of the Arkadian shepherds.

In very ancient times, the shepherds of Arkadia had their own god: goat-footed Pan, whose pipes breathed life into nature and who hunted the nymphs through the pine forests of Mt Mainalo. At that time, they say, the region was inhabited by the indigenous population of 'Pelasgians'.

It was believed by these ancient people that the first human beings were born of the Great Mother, Gaea. Important cities grew up here in the historical period: Tegea, Mantineia, Orchomenos, Megalopolis. Until Roman times, when it went into decline, Arkadia was able to maintain a degree of autonomy from the warlike Dorians who had conquered the rest of the Peloponnese. The large number of monasteries on Mt Parnon demonstrates the deep influence of Byzantium and Christianity. Under the 'Franks' Arkadia was divided into five baronies. In 1458, it passed into the hands of the Turks.

No conqueror was ever really able to dominate Arkadia. They were driven out by the rugged mountains and the even more rugged inhabitants. The Greeks paid their taxes to the Turks, but built an administrative centre of their own: Tripoli, then known as Hydropolitsa or Droboglitsa. A Turkish pasha was installed there, but the Greeks high in the mountains or down in the plain of Megalopoli continued to live much as they pleased. There were secret schools to teach the children the rudiments of Greek learning and to keep alive the Christian faith. Some of those schools can still be today, at the St John the Baptist Monastery near Stemnitsa, in the Monastery of Our Lady 'Sfyrida' at Vitina, and at the Monastery of the Dormition 'Filosophou' in Dimitsana, where the famous 'Dimitsana School' came into being. Dimitsana had gunpowder factories as well, and both they and the school were important in paving the way for the rising of 1821. Tripoli was soon liberated, and became the headquarters of the entire independence movement.

And so we come to the Arkadia of more recent times. The Arkadians were skilled and painstaking workers in stone, wood, silver and gold. They were able to accumulate power and wealth; particularly those of them who went to Athens to practise their crafts, though they never forgot the places from which they had set out. As people of determination themselves, their stories and sayings show their disdain for those who cannot make up their minds to do what is right, waste time and end up as losers. "He ate the onions, he got a beating and he paid the debt as well!", they say. The story behind this is of a man in the old days who owed money to a Turk. The Turk gave him the choice of eating forty onions, taking forty blows or paying the debt. He chose the onions; he ate twenty or so, but could manage no more, and so the Turk began to beat him. After twenty blows or so, he could stand it no longer and cried out that he would pay the debt!.

There are other stories which tell us something of the way of life that developed in more modern times. The Arkadians, for example, have little patience with skinflints:

"How much does iron cost?"
"Sixty pence".
"Weigh me out a farthing's worth of needles".

Nor can they stand liars and those who spread false rumours:

"How sweet that milk is!"
"How do you know?"
"My uncle saw someone drinking some on the other side of the river!"

87

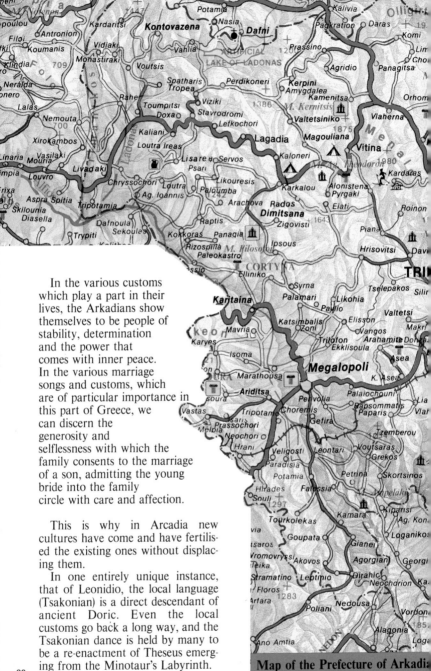

In the various customs which play a part in their lives, the Arkadians show themselves to be people of stability, determination and the power that comes with inner peace. In the various marriage songs and customs, which are of particular importance in this part of Greece, we can discern the generosity and selflessness with which the family consents to the marriage of a son, admitting the young bride into the family circle with care and affection.

This is why in Arcadia new cultures have come and have fertilised the existing ones without displacing them.

In one entirely unique instance, that of Leonidio, the local language (Tsakonian) is a direct descendant of ancient Doric. Even the local customs go back a long way, and the Tsakonian dance is held by many to be a re-enactment of Theseus emerging from the Minotaur's Labyrinth.

Map of the Prefecture of Arkadia

13. Astros · Leonidi
(50 kms)

After Kiveri, the coastal road from the Argolid continues to the south to **Paralio Astros**, a charming resort village with, at Nisi, the ruins of a Venetian castle. The main road continues south west and soon enters Astros.

The existence of a town on the site of **Astros** can be traced back as far as the 13th century BC, and its name seems to derive from the ancient word 'asty' (city) which was then corrupted to 'Astri' and later Astros. One of the statues found in the ruins of the ancient city is now in the Athens Archaeological Museum. This is a caryatid in the same style as

Phedias' famous Amazon, and is the only ancient copy to have retained its head. The town also played a leading part in the War of Independence. Astros Museum has exhibits of inscriptions from the villa of Herod Atticus (on the site of the Loukou Convent), marble statues of gods from the Classical period, inscriptions, pottery, small items from various periods, etc. The countryside around Astros is extremely fertile, and trees, flowers and undergrowth are all watered by the spring known as 'Mana'. The area is famous for its peaches, while it also produces olive oil, wheat and other cereals, pears, etc. Astros makes fine rugs, with intricate weaving and pleasant designs. The anniversary of the National Convention is the occasion for a two-day feast. There is also a

Paralio Astrous seen from its Venetian castle.

The beach at Tyros.

four-day feast to to mark the Ascension, in May. Lake Moustos, nearby, has plenty of fish for the amateur fisherman and is popular with hunters during the winter.

Among the interesting things to be seen in the country around is the Convent of Loukous, (Transfiguration) where, in a well-preserved 11th century Byzantine church, is kept an icon of the Saviour which is said to be miraculous.

Soon after leaving Astros, the road south comes to a fork. The left turning takes us to the pretty village of **Oreini Meligou**, on the thickly-forested slopes of Mt Parnon. It also leads to Lake Moustos, and a spring whose water is supposed to be good for sufferers from rheumatism and arthritis.

The other fork leads south east to **Korakovouni**, which hides the ruins of a Venetian castle among its plane trees. The Avourou gorge, near the village, is popular with hunters. A small cave with stalactites lies nearby, and fine views are to be had from Vrysi and Petsopos.

The village of **Ayios Andreas**, further to the south, is also pretty, and we can descend east from there to its beach, **Paralia Ayiou Andrea**, amongst olive trees, orange trees and lemon trees.

Some scholars have identified Ayios Andreas as the site of ancient Brasiae or Brasias, which is referred to in the myth of Semele and Dionysus. There are remains of a very ancient acropolis on the cliff above the village — the ruins may go back as far as Pelasgian times, and other Pelasgian remains can be seen in the surrounding area. Graves have also been found, from various periods, and chains and other signs that ships were moored in the mouth of the river Brasiatos (known today as Zarbanitsa).

The nearby Orthokostas Monastery (Transfiguration) has a marvellous 12th century chapel with Byzantine wall-paintings and a Turkish tower stands nearby.

The road carries on to the South, beside the sea. From the pretty village of **Paralia Tyros** a minor road to the right (west) leads up the hill to **Tyros**, which preserves the name of an ancient city. The villages of **Sapounakeïka, Pera Melana** and **Pragmatefti** lie beside the sea, after which the road follows the fine Sambatiki coast as far as the turning to the west into Leonidi.

Leonidi takes its name from a little church to St Leonidas, which is mentioned in a chrysobull of the Emperor Andronikos Komninos of 1282.

The town is built on the site of the ancient city of **Prasiae**, on the banks of a river which is usually dry in spring and summer. The town is closed in on three sides by mountains, the fourth side being open in the direction of the sea. There are a few bridges linking the houses on the two sides of the riverbed.

It is the capital of the province of Kynouria (also known as Tsakonia), and its inhabitants, along with those of the surrounding countryside, speak the peculiar Tsakonian dialect, which has traces of the ancient Doric language. The local 'tsakonikos' dance and the local costume, known as 'tzoumbes', also preserve Doric austerity. The rugs made in the district are handsome and hard-wearing.

Remains of the ancient acropolis and Pelasgian walls have been found on a hill above the town, and the churches of St Demetrius (12th century) and St Athanasius (11th century) stand among the ancient ruins. The church of St Kyriaki (16th century) is also worth a visit. The Museum, which is housed in the High School, contains finds from the temple of Apollo Tyrites and from Mycenean graves at Vaskina. There is a Folk Art Museum with some particularly impressive examples of wood carving.

The road leads east for 4 km before coming to **Plaka**, a fine and extensive beach. In the surrounding countryside, the visitor will be impressed

Leonidio, capital of Tsakonia, maintains ma

by the imposing sites of the monasteries of Elona (of Our Lady, at the base of a cliff) and Sintzas (to St Nicholas). The hinterland is rich in game and the sea ideal for spearfishing.

To the west of Leonidi, the road runs first to the Elons nunnery and then climbs into the forest of Mt Parnon, running through the upland village of Kosmas before descending to the historic town of Yeraki (see page 196).

South of Leonidi and Plaka, a road directs to **Tsitalia** and another road to the beautiful **Poulithra**, with its ultimate destination Laconia and the imposing town of Yeraki (see p. 196).

Elona Nunnery.

its ancient traditions.

14. Tripoli - Tegea (10 kms)

The old road from Argos continues towards Tripoli (see p. 85) along the slopes of Mt Parthenio. To the left, on a mound, are the ruins of the strong medieval fortress of Mouchli, which was built after the walls of Amycle were razed but was itself destroyed in 1460.

We come to the village of **Ayiorgitika**, where a fine Archaic statue, currently in the Athens Archaeological Museum, was found.

We soon pass through **Steno**, cross the Sarantapotamos river and enter **Tripoli**.

The town stands almost in the centre of the Peloponnese, at an altitude of 650 metres, on the Arcadian plateau. Although the plain itself is almost treeless and the climate is harsh, the mountainsides around are far from bereft of vegetation. Tripoli itself is an important commercial and administrative centre.

The town's history begins at some point in the 15th century, when, after the fall of Constantinople to the Turks (1453) small groups of local people from the towns which had been destroyed by the invaders (Mouchli, Davia, etc.) began to settle in the plain.

A Turkish fort known as Drobolitsa is mentioned in 1467, and this became corrupted to Tripolitsa and a city began to grow up. In the end, it was further corrupted to give the form which we know today. Travellers' accounts in the 18th century accord it little importance.

Like the rest of the Peloponnese, Tripoli took part in the unsuccessful rising against the Turks under Russian Admiral Orloff in 1770, and the town was severely punished.

But soon afterwards Tripoli was made the administrative headquarters of the Turks in the Peloponnese, and especially under the governorship of Veli Pasha, son of Ali Pasha of Ioannina, at the start of the 19th century, much economic progress began to be made, particularly in light industry. This was largely the work of tradesmen and craftsmen from Epirus and other areas who settled in the district at about this time.

During the 1821 Revolution, the Greek forces besieged the town, where more than 40,000 Turks from the surrounding area had taken refuge. The Greeks finally took the town in September 1821 but held it for only four years. The Turks and Egyptians of Ibrahim destroyed it thoroughly the second time, and it had to be rebuilt after the country's freedom had been won.

Now it is one of the most important commercial centres in the Peloponnese. Its Archaeological Museum is of some importance.

Tripoli is an important communications centre, with roads spreading out like the spokes of a wheel to all parts of the Peloponnese. Indeed, it is hard to avoid Tripoli when travelling in the area.

A main road and minor road leave Tripoli and cross the plain of **Tegea**. The main road runs in a southerly direction into Lakonia.

Tripolis, the capital of Arkadia. Above: the Malliaropouleio Theater and the statue of Kolokotronis on horseback. Below: the Courthouse in Areos Square.

Seven kms south of Tripoli, between the villages of **Ag. Sostis**, **Episkopi**, **Akra**, **Stadio** and **Alea**, is the region of **ancient Tegeatida**.

Alea (also known as Piali) has an archaeological museum, which contains, among other things, prehistoric pottery, sculpture and architectural members from the temple of Alean Athena (with two torsos of Nike Apteros from the workshop of Skopas), pottery from the Classical period, Hellenistic figurines, small copper votive offerings, etc.

According to tradition, Tegea was founded either by Aleos, son of Aphidas, or by Epaminondas. There were eight demes in the area, and Aphidas unified these for greater protection against the Spartans. Thus a city with a strong acropolis grew up in around the 9th century B.C. near the modern village of Akra. Aleos was responsible for introducing a common religion and building the temple of Alean Athena.

According to Pausanias, this was the largest temple in the Peloponnese, in the Doric style, and built wholly of marble, with decorations by Skopas. Its beauty was reputed to compete with that of the temple of Zeus at Olympia. It is said that both Orestes and Pausanias found refuge in the sanctuary of the temple.

Nothing remains today except the podium of the later Doric temple and some architectural members. The temple had narthex, recess and opisthodomos (vestibule at the back). At the back of the recess stood the ivory statue of Alean Athena, and on her right and left, marble statues of Asclepius and Hygeia. The pediments of the temple bore scenes from

Tegea: the head of the goddess Hyggeia, from the temple of Athena Alea (National Archaeological Museum).

mythology (the hunting of the Calydonian Boar, the quarrel of Telephus and Achilles), of which some parts are on display in the museum.

Tegea (which was also notable for its civic facilities —agora, marble theatre, stadium for the local Alean Games, etc.) defended the independence of Arcadia for many centuries before having to give in to Sparta in 469. Tegea sent troops to fight at the side of the other Greeks during the Persian Wars, and joined the Arcadian League (Koinon of the Arcadians) after the battle of Leuctra (371). Later —in 235— it allied itself with the Aetolians, and under the rule of Macedon joined the Achaean League. It became insignificant and was finally destroyed in the 4th century AD by Alaric's Vizigoths. The Byzantines soon rebuilt it, however, and made it the seat of the Bishop of Amykles (Nikliou). But it fell from power again after the 7th century, and was destroyed once more in 1295, its position being taken over by the fortress of Mouchli. The power and might of the ancient city, however, are attested to by the participation of its warriors and heroes in feats and campaigns in mythology and by the existence of Tegean colonies in Cyprus and Crete.

Today, there is an attractive modern village by the name of Tegea. The area is intensively farmed and there are crops of all kinds.

Near the Agora of Tegea, in the village of **Episkopi**, there was a theatre built in c. 175 B.C. by Antiochus III Epiphanes. Within it were found the ruins of a Byzantine church of the Virgin, which was restored to replace that of the 11th or 12th century which served as the cathedral of Nikliou, as Tegea was called in the Middle Ages. In front of the church can be seen the remains of medieval walls and a mosaic floor (5th century) with symbolic representations of the four rivers of Paradise, the 12 months, etc. Around the church there is a fine park with pines and other trees with a tourist pavilion.

A six-day feast around 15 August, with competitions and a market, preserves a tradition whose origins must be very ancient.

Tegea: the temple of Athena Alea.

15. Tripoli - Megalopoli
(35 kms)

The main road to Kalamata leaves Tripoli to the south west.

A turning to the right at 6.5 kms brings us on to a minor road to **Valtetsi**, a historic village built on a rocky slope and surrounded by mountains. On 25 April and 12-13 May 1821 two decisive battles were fought here between Greeks and Turks, won by the former. The battles are acted out each year (on 12-13 May), thus quickening in the mind these feats of Kolokotronis and his men, which improved the Greeks' morale and opened the way for the conquest of Tripoli.

The next turning off the Kalamata road to the left, east leads to **Pallantio**. Between Pallantio and **Evandros**, to the south, lie the remains of ancient Pallantion, near Lake Taka, one of the oldest and most famous cities in Arcadia. According to mythology, the city was founded by Pallas, son of Lykaon.

Another old legend has it that Evander, a god or perhaps a demon from the circle of Pan (god of Arcadian shepherds), who was the son of Hermes and Thetis (daught of Ladon), set off from Pallantion with some companions before the Trojan War and landed in Italy. He built a settlement on a hill outside what later became Rome, and the hill was named Palatine in honour of his native city. Thus, when the Romans invaded Greece they allowed Pallantion of Arcadia to remain a free city.

After the turning for Pallantion, the road to Kalamata runs up to the Kaloyerikos pass, at 800 metres, and then twists down into the plain again.

At about the 15th kilometre, we come to the Frankovrysi spring, which the ancients believed to be the source of the rivers Alpheus and Eurotas.

This is the start of the plain of Asea, as it was called in antiquity, or Sapiko, to use its medieval name (also known today as 'Sapolivado').

Near the 17th kilometre is the settlement of **Kato Asea**, and above the village the ruins of the ancient acropolis can be picked out.

A minor road leads off uphill to the right (north west) and enters **Asea**, a thickly-vegetated and well-watered area, which lies at the foot of Mount Profitis Elias (which may be the ancient Korphios). Traces of temples of Athena Sotira and Poseidon have been found on the peak of the mountain.

From the modern village a minor road climbs up north-west to **Arachamites** (760 metres), near which there is a model farm of the Monastery of the Transfiguration.

The main road twists down into Megalopoli — care should be taken on the bends.

Near the last bend, to the right, is the Monastery of Our Lady 'Makrysiou', and a minor road leads to the village of the same name (also known as Salesi) where the Greek leader Captain Zacharias fought victoriously against a superior Turkish force during the War of Liberation.

Megalopoli is an administrative and commercial centre for the surrounding agricultural region, which produces mostly cereals and animal products.

The town stands almost in the middle of a small plain, near its ancient namesake (the name mears "large city"). It is encircled by mountains — Mainalos to the north, Lykaion to the north west, and Taiyetos to the south. The river Alpheus passes to the west and south, and the Elissonas (or Barboutsiana, or Daria River) to the north. The ancient city was built at the junction of the two rivers, thus creating an important military and administrative centre at a time of general decline in Greece (371-368 BC).

Megalopolis attrackted settlers from all over Arcadia. There were temples to Lycaean Zeus, the Mother of the Gods, Asclepius, and others, of which some ruins have come to light together with those of other buildings (Stoa of Philippos, Stoa of Myropolis, a santuary of Zeus Soter and a Bouleuterion).

The river runs through the archaeological site.

The ancient theatre, which has seats for more than 20,000, was the largest in Greece, and has excellent acoustics. The ancient drama is revived occasionally there in summer.

The main road some 20 kms to the south west of Megalopoli enters the Prefecture of Messenia (see p. 160).

The theatre at Megalopolis, the largest in ancient Greece.

16. Megalopoli - Ano Karyes (23 kms)

The main road, which leads South-West out of Megalopolis towards Kalamata, soon (2 kms) meets a minor road to the right (west) which runs through a fine oak forest.

A little further on, at the village of **Apiditsa**, the road forks, one branch going to the left (southwest) to **Isari**, finely situated at an altitude of 850 metres, with an impressive view of the mountains of Arkadia and Taiyetos.

The road continues through a wooded area, ending at **Vasta**. Just outside the village is the Church of St Theodora, with a domed roof, a spring beneath the foundations and 17 trees growing on the roof.

The other branch of the Apiditsa fork leads West to the ruins of **Lykosoura**. The city was built on a hill, with a panoramic view of the plain of Megalopolis and is very ancient — Pausanias says that it was *"the first city on which the sun shone"*. This was a holy city for the Arcadians, and very ancient gods were worshipped here. The religion of the area also had deep roots; remains have been found of a temple to Despoina, a deity of the underworld who some scholars have identified with Persephone. However, the real name of Despoina, which simply means 'the Mistress', has not come down to us, since even in the 2nd century AD people were afraid to tell it to the uninitiated. There are also traces of altars to Demeter, Despoina and the Great Mother. There was another temple to Despoina nearby, built in the 4th century BC.

The Museum is notable for its fragmentary sculptures of Demeter and Despoina by Damaphon, a 2nd century Messenian sculptor, inscriptions, clay pots, sculpted decorations, etc.

From the archaeological site, the road turns north and enters the modern village of **Lykosoura**.

A little further to the north we come to **Lykaio**, 600 metres up with a fine spring in the centre, and the road ends at **Ano Karyes**. The village, which stands at an altitude of 850 metres, has fine mountain scenery, with six springs, walnut trees, abundant flowers and grass.

Ano Karyes is the starting-point for the ascent of Mt Lykaion (1,421 metres), an interesting walk of about

The little chapel of St Theodora, with seventeen (17!) trees growing on its roof.

Leontari: the Byzantine church of the Holy Apostles.

an hour. At about 1,200 metres we come to small plateau, known to the locals as Elliniko, where traces have been found of a shrine to Pan, god of the Arcadian shepherds.

Ruins of a hippodrome and a stadium have also been discovered. Here the Lycaean games, in honour of Zeus, were held — games which pre-date the Panathenian Games of Athens. The base of a column may be seen a little further up the mountain, near the chapel of the Prophet Elias.

In ancient times two columns stood here, ornamented with golden eagles, at the foot of a hillock which was a shrine to Zeus. Sacrifices were made on the altar even human sacrifices, according to some accounts. The myths say that Lycaon sacrificed an infant there, only to see it turned into a wolf by Zeus.

17. Megalopoli - Dyrrachi
(34 kms)

A charming side-road leads out of Megalopoli to the south, into an area notable for its thick vegetation, pleasant villages and monasteries, but famous above all for the part it played in the Greeks' struggle for freedom.

Four kilometres from Megalopoli we come to **Yefira**, where there is a bridge over the Alpheus. At the 11th kilometre to the south, at a height of 540 metres, stands **Leontari**, which was a town of importance in the 14th century, when it was the seat of the Despots of the Morea (Peloponnese). The town's castle, whose ruins stand on a steep hill overlooking it, was built then.

Under the Turks, Leontari was the capital of its sow separate province. It took part in the abortive Orloff revolt (1770), and was severely punished by the Turks. When the Revolution broke out, many of the local people offered their lives and their fortunes to the cause and heroic pages of history were written here.

The Byzantine church of the Apostles, 14th century, with wall-paintings (for many years covered by a coat of whitewash), has been described as one of the finest in Greece. The churches of St Athanasius (in the Byzantine style, 12th century, with partially destroyed wall-paintings), and St Nicon (with wall-paintings) are also of interest.

A minor road leads south west from Leontari, through **Kalyvia** with a turn to Veligosti and Paradisia. At four kilometres south from Leontari we enter **Potamia**, which affords the opportunity of a visit to the Monastery of Our Lady 'Houn-tallou', built on a rock half an hour's walk away.

Nearby is the interesting church of the Monastery of St Nicon.

The road continues along the valley of the river Xerilas (in ancient times, Karnion), through the villages of **Kambohori**, **Kamara** and **Kato Yanneïka**. Kamara was the base of the Revolutionary hero Bouras. Yanneïka, near the banks of the Xerilas, has a spot where a spring bubbles up in an idyllic setting.

The road climbs southwards outside the village of Kato Yanneïka. This road passes near the gorge of Kouvaras, with numerous springs, about 16 kilometres from Leontari,

where there is an interesting cave.

We then pass through the pretty village of **Ano Yanneïka** (1,000 metres). The pine-clad peak of Yanniotikos Agiolias · towers over the village, and a large rock, which can be seen from the road, was Kolokotronis' vantage point during the battle of Drabala.

Further to the south stands **Dyrrachi**, built at a height of 840 metres. It is an attractive and verdant village, divided into four separate settlements. There are fine pine-clad mountain slopes all around. Ruins of the medieval fort of Palaiopyrgos and the Monastery of St Nicon may be seen in the area.

The route from Dyrrachi to the historic **Monastery of St. George 'Rekitsas'**, at an altitude of 1,200 m., is truly unforgettable. The monastery itself, which had a secret school, was the training ground for many of the heroes of the Greek Revolution, such as Papaflessas, Zacharias, Anagnostaras, (Papayeorgiou), Kolokotronis, Nikitaras and the Flessas and Kefalas families.

The church is cruciform, with fine well-paintings of 1714, the work of 'Michael Pediotis Cretan', as we are informed by an inscription.

A minor road leads from Dyrrachi to the east, through **Neochori** and on South to the Sparta-Kalamata road (see p. 183).

Karytaina and

18. Megalopoli - Karytaina
(21 kms)

A main road leads out of Megalopoli to the north.

About 20 kilometres from Megalopoli we enter **Karytaina**, an impressive village whose easily-fortified position made it important from the Middle Ages to the time of the Revolution. In 1209, it was created capital of Hugo de Bruyéres' barony, and he built the castle there slightly later. The Chronicle of the Morea is fulsome in its praise of his son Geoffrey, whom it calls 'lord of Karytaina'.

The town and its castle passed through the hands of many masters

...edieval castle.

in the centuries which followed: Franks, Byzantines, Turks, Venetians and Turks again.

The main road twists on to the West, towards Ileia.

We soon cross the river Alpheus, at a point where there is an old arched bridge, with an inscription on the base stating that it was repaired in 1439 by Raoul Manuel Melikis, a Palaeologue official.

At the 23rd kilometre from Megalopoli, a small road to the left leads to a Turkish mosque and the village of **Kourouniou**. The road continues through fine scenery, with the Alpheus flowing in a deep ravine to the right, up to **Theisoa** (Lavda) at a height of 400 metres. The main road continues to Andritsaina (see p. 155).

19. Tripoli - Astros
(Via Ayios Petros 46 kms)

Two roads (see p. 94), one a main one and the other more minor, lead south from Tripoli to the Tegea plain.

The main one, continuing south, leads to the Lakonia region and Sparta, while the smaller road takes us to the south east, with imposing views of the bulk of Mt Parnon (Malevos), one of the most thickly-forested Greek mountains. The river Tanos can be seen to the left, as can villages in the Kastri area — Karatoula, Nea Hora, Kakavos, etc.

At a point 14 kilometres south of Tripoli, after the village of Rizes, the minor road divides. The right (eastward) branch leads to the villages of **Ayia Sophia, Prosilia, Ano Doliana** and the town of **Astros**. This is the shortest way to the sea.

Longer, but much more interesting, is the left branch (to the south east), which climbs round bends and branches off at 22 kilometres from Tripoli to the attractive village of Kato Doliana, famous in the Greek War of Independence of 1821.

The old monastery of St John the Baptist (Kastriou), whose large cave was used as a hospital and a refuge for numerous Greek families during the Revolution, can be seen in the plain of Xirokambi.

At 28 kilometres, after **Mesorachi,** the road enters **Ayios Nikolaos**, chief village of the Kastriou region.

Thirty five kilometres from Tripoli, we come to **Ayios Petros**, at an altitude of 940 metres. The village is well-watered and has a wide variety of trees, including apple, pear, plum and cherry trees, chestnuts and planes, as well as bushes and other greenery. Cypresses, pines, firs and oak trees may be seen towards the peaks of Mt Parnon.

Ayios Petros is a medieval town, and under the Turks and Venetians it was the capital of a province. Apart from the church of the Apostles Peter and Paul, the church of the local patron saint (St Nilus) is also worth a visit. There are interesting feasts at both churches in May and June.

The road continues east. We soon reach the Nunnery of the Dormition of the Virgin 'Malevi', built around 1600.

Before this there was another nunnery, at a point higher up where there is a spring and some ruins of a church. Even earlier the monastery stood still highr on the slopes.

The nunnery was a favourite haunt of freedom fighters during the Turkish occupation, and a battle fought here in 1786 ended in victory for the Greeks under Zacharias Barbitsiotis and Thanasis Karambelas-Verveniotis. As a reprisal, the Turks laid waste the monastery. During the Wars of Independence, many freedom fighters sought sanctuary here.

The road continues to the north east, down to the coastal plain. We pass through **Oreini Meligou** and enter Astros (see p. 90).

20. Tripoli · Dimitsana
(53 kms)

A minor road leads north west from Tripoli. We pass through **Silimna** (880 metres), which was the rallying-point during the Orloff revolt in 1770. The ancient city of **Lycoa** stood on the slopes of Mt Mainalos, opposite.

At 10 kilometres, a road to the left (west) leads to **Tselepakos** and from there to **Zarakova**, 950 metres up the side of Mt Mainalos.

The main road continues among pine trees. At the 15th kilometre we reach **Davia**. Nearby, at Palaiokastro, are the ruins of the ancient Arcadian city of Mainalos and a medieval castle.

The Lousios is a tributary of the Alpheios.

A minor road leads from Davia to the west and soon, at a height of 1,150 metres, enters **Chrysovitsi**. The village is set in a pine forest, and there is a saw-mill.

The pine-woods had a reputation even in ancient times, when, according to the myths, Arktos, the beautiful daughter of Lycaon and Kallisto, was caught there by Zeus, who had his wicked way with her. She had a son, Arcadas, who gave his name to the area. Hera, out of jealousy, turned the girl into a bear, and Arcadas, when he grew up —not knowing anything of his origin—killed the bear in the forest. Zeus then turned mother and son into two constellations — Ursa Major and Ursa Minor.

A little way before we reach Stemnitsa (Ipsous), a turning to the left leads to **Elliniko, Syrna, Psari, Paliomiri** and **Pavlia** before joining the Megalopoli-Karytaina road.

After Elliniko there is a fork to the right. The minor road which branches off goes to **Atsilochos**, at a height of 580 metres, near which the remains of **Ancient Gortys** have come to light.

Of special interest are the ruins of the baths, of the temple of Asclepius, which contained a statue of Hygeia by Skopas, and the remaining sections of the polygonal walls of the acropolis. A bridge of ancient stone may be seen over the river Lousios, a tributary of the Alpeus, on the bank of which is a Byzantine church (St Andrew), while nearby is the church of the old Kalami Monastery (to Our Lady).

Following the main route after the turning for Elliniko, the road climbs north west and enters **Stemnitsa (Ipsous)**.

The ample greenery of the village contrasts pleasantly with the pines on Mt Klinitsa, and the village stands at a height of 1,050 metres, near the site of an ancient city of the same name.

The two small churches in the castle, St Nicholas (renovated in 1589) and Our Lady 'Bafero' (perhaps built in 1640) have high quality wall-paintings in a good state of preservation. The Church of the Three Hierarchs, near the school, preserves wall-paintings of 1715 by Petros Pediotis.

The Lousios gorge and the monastery of St John the Baptist.

Stemnitsa has scores of fine houses, most of which are restored or newrly-built using traditional materials and techniques.

In a beautiful spot to the south west of Stemnitsa, in the gorge of the river Lousios, stands the Monastery of St John the Baptist, where the relics of St Athanasius, bishop of Christianoupolis, are kept. The monastery is reputed to have been built in 1167 by the Emperor Manuel Comnenos.

The road leaves Stemnitsa to the west and soon turns north.

A minor road to the right (east) leads to the mountain summer resort of **Zygovisti**, at 1,200 metres, near which is the Aimyalo monastery.

Historic Dimitsana was of importance during the war of Independence of 1821.

Dimitsana lies some 54 kilometres to the north west of Tripoli. The town stands at 950 metres, in a verdant area, with fine views of the Arcadian mountains, the river Lousios, where Zeus is reputed to have bathred, and the plain of Megalopolis.

Near the town have been found ruins of Cyclopean walls and classical buildings which may have belonged to the acropolis of the ancient city of Teuthis. The town was at its zenith in the Middle Ages, first being mentioned in Patriarchal documents in 963.

In 1764, the monk Hatzi Agapios (Asimakis Leonardos) founded a school there, to become known as the 'School of Greek Letters', and set up a library to which that of the nearby Monastery of the Philosophos was transferred. The school gave a grounding in letters to many important Greeks, among them 70 church leaders, and was a centre for revolutionary activities against the Turks. The Patriarch Gregory V and Bishop Yermanos of Patras, important figures in the Revolution, both attended the school, and the gunpowder factory of the Spiliotopoulos family kept the revolutionaries in cartridges — indeed, the shortage of paper for these was so great that valuable books from the library had to be used.

The Museum in Dimitsana preserves Mycenean pottery, Archaic sculpture, clay and copper figurines, vessels and sculpture from the Hellenistic and Roman periods.

109

There is also a Folk Museum with examples of weaving, looms, metalwork and other superb examples of folk crafts. The 19th century building of the Municipal Library contains relics of Bishop Yermanos.

Dimitsana is an ideal centre for excursions to shady glades and pine forests.

To the west, we have the 10th century Monastery of the Philosopher, founded by Ioannis Lambardopoulos, known as 'the Philosophos', official at the court of the Emperor Nicephorus Phocas, its principal purpose being to Hellenise and Christianise the Slavs of the area. The first monastery was built in the hollow of a rock in the Lousios gorge, on a spot so inaccessible the it could only be reached with the help of ladders. At the beginning of the 17th century, it was transferred to a location more easy to reach. It has a church of the Dormition, with fine wall-paintings.

A minor road to the west and then south leads to the pretty and verdant village of **Zatouna**, at 900 metres.

Another road, leading north, and before entering the village of **Karkalou**, where it joins the Tripoli-Vitina-Pyrgos road, has a fork to the pretty and verdant village of **Servou**.

The church of St Foteini at Mantineia, in modern architectural style.

21. Tripoli - Vytina
(45 kms)

The main road leaves Tripoli to the north, with the pine-clad slopes Mainalos on the left. We soon pass the Monastery of Epano Chrepa.

Out on the plain of Milia, 10 kilometres from Tripoli, a minor road climbs off to the right (northeast) to the ruins of **Ancient Mantinea** and its acropolis. The ruins stand on the hill known locally as Gortsouli.

The city was first mentioned by Homer, and is supposed to have taken its name from Mantineas, son of Lycaon. It seems, at that time, to have been a loose federation of four or five settlements, which sent warriors to Troy. According to Strabo, their unification was the work of Argos, which wished to use them to counter-balance the power of nearby Tegea. Polybius is full of praise for Mantinea. Shortly before the Persian wars, Mantinea recognised the sway of Sparta, on whose side it fought in the wars.

In the Peloponnesian Wars, the city fought with the League, but later left it. Then it fought Tegea, was allied with Athens, was forced to side with Sparta again after 418, was once again destroyed in its attempts to rid itself of its Spartan overlords, and so on. Epaminondas rebuilt it in 371. Mantinea was Sparta's ally again and, with it, was defeated by Epaminondas in 362.

Among the ruins we can see the theatre, the Agora, temples, and other buildings. The city had an unusual sanctuary of Poseidon, which did not have doors, but a red woollen thread across the door openings. The temple contained a salt spring, and only the priest of Poseidon had the right to enter. Myths tell us that King Aipylos once cut the thread and entered, only to come out blinded some time later and die.

The main road continues north west. We pass the pretty village of **Kapsia**, and come to a crossroads.

The branch of the road to the west leads to the skiing centre of Mainalos (at 1,000 m., 30 kilometres from Tripoli).

Twenty six kilometres along the main road from Tripoli, we come to **Levidi**, a large village at a height of 750 metres.

The landscape is most attractive. There is a picturesque chapel to Our Lady on a hill nearby, to the east, on the site of a sanctuary to Artemis Hymnia, respected throughout Arcadia.

A road leaves Levidi to the north east, and soon comes to a fork to the right (east) which leads to the pretty village of **Artemisio** (Kakouri) and, further on, to the ruins of Ancient Mantinea.

Shortly after this fork we come to the ruins of **Ancient Orchomenos**, a town of great importance in the area as far back as the Mycenean age.

Its strong acropolis is reputed to have been built by yet another son of Lycaon, Orchomenos.

The city was important up to the fifth century BC, and had, on some occasions, been the seat of the king of Arcadia. The town's significance can be seen from the fact that it minted its own coins into the Roman period.

A little further, 13 kilometres from Tripoli, we come to the Kandila Monastery, at 1,050 metres.

The road descends to **Kandila** and in the Prefecture of Argolis.

From Levidi, the main Tripoli-Vytina road continues north west. We soon come to the attractive village of **Vlacherna** (at an attitude of 1,100 metres), with the historic monastery of the same name north of the village.

Nearby, at Kastro, is where historians reckon was the site of the fortress of Bezeniko (1463). The site is occupied today by the Eleousa Monastery, and shows the ruins of six churches, storehouses and underground chambers.

After Vlacherna to the west there is a fork. The right-hand fork soon encounters a minor road to the left, which leads to the Lados valley and its villages, while the main road continues north to Kalavryta.

The left-hand fork turns south west, along fir-clad slopes. Soon it enters **Vytina**, one of the most idyllic and famous Greek mountain resorts, at a height of 1,000 metres.

There are modern tourist amenities. The thick forests of Mt Mainalo give Vytina a healthy and invigorating climate as well as providing the raw material for local arts and crafts. Wood-carving is a local tradition. The site was well-known even in ancient times, when it was associated with Pan and other Arcadian deities.

During the Revolution, it was an educational centre, with a secret school which initially operated at the Theotokos (Kernitsa) Monastery nearby and later moved into the village itself. These activities were helped by the fact that no Turks ever settled in Vytina.

Nearby (to the north west) are the remains of the old town of **Kernitsa**, which was famous for its many churches. One of the town's 12 hills preserves the church of St Nicholas, and 4 kilometres away from Vytina is the finely-sited Byzantine monastery of Our Lady 'Theotokos'.

From Vytina a minor road leads south east to Alonistaina, Piana and Davia, and from there to Tripoli.

The road continues downhill through a thickly-wooded area.

The scattered remains of Arcadian Orchomenos.

The Monastery of Our Lady, Kernitsa.

In a beautiful gorge at a height of 690 m., **Alonistaina** (famous from the time of the Franks) rises before us. Surrounded by the fir-clad slopes of Mt Mainalo, nature has made it an ideal holiday resort. Sheltered from the wind at a height of 1,120 metres, the so-called 'Alonistaina saddle' is a place of unique beauty.

To the south, at a height of 1,050 metres, is the village of **Piana** above the green valley of Falantho, through which run the waters of the Elisson (Davia River). There are remains of a medieval castle and of the ancient city of Dipaea.

Further south is **Davia**, and 20 kilometres further on, Tripoli.

22. Vytina - Langadia
(27 kms)

The multi-storey houses of Langadia.

The main road continues to the south of Vytina and soon turns west.

The route takes us through fine scenery, with plenty of greenery. We pass a spring next to the road, and, at the 50th kilometre, we come to **Petrovouni**, where there are a few remains of **Ancient Methydrion**, which had a temple to Poseidon Hypios.

A minor road leads off to the right (north west), and soon brings us to **Magouliana**, summer residence of the Villehardouin family of nobles.

Another beautiful spot is the area around **Valtetsiniko**, at 1,050 metres a little further on. There is rich vegetation and ample water from a spring. The village is famous for its production of wooden furniture in the traditional style.

Some scholars contend that the village stands on the site of Ancient **Lousoi**. The present name dates back to 1204.

The church of St George, built in 1850, is regarded by experts as a masterpiece of its kind —its dome is not supported on columns, and appears to be flying. The local Dinopoulos brothers carved the wonderful screen, the paintings on which are the work of the artist Myronas, from Tinos. Another screen by the same brothers can be seen in the church of St Theodore (1835). A tall medieval tower still has tenants in the ground floor, although the upper storey is ruinous. It is known as 'The Tower of the Despots' (of the Morea), by whom it is supposed to have been built.

Close to the village, to the north west, is the Monastery of the Dormition of the Virgin, which has a 16th century church with fine wall-paintings.

There is a pretty little wood nearby. The remains of a Byzantine fort can be seen on Aimilianos hill, from the top of which there is a panoramic view of Mt Chelmos (Aroania) and Mt Erymanthos.

The two churches of St Nicholas and the Ascension are built in a two-storeyed cave near Valtetsiniko, and have 14th and 15th century wall-paintings. They were destroyed by Ibrahim's troops.

The road continues north west and soon joins the minor road which began just outside Vlacherna and led down through the Ladonas valley and its villages.

The main road continues to the south west and enters the picturesque village of **Karkalou**, at 810 metres.

Langadia is a fine town, standing in a natural amphitheatre, 72 kilometres from Tripoli. The site is verdant and there is running water everywhere. The inhabitants are famed for their building skills, which find expression in the tall houses of the village.

This road then forks at **Stavrodromi**, the main road continuing into the Ileia region, in the direction of Ancient Olympia (see p. 154).

23. The Ladonas Dam

A minor road leads north from Stavrodromi, through **Vyziki** (740 metres) and soon reaches **Tropaia**, also built amphitheatrically on the slopes of Mt Ayios Yeorgios. As a resort town, it is visited by many Greeks and foreign tourists each year.

A medieval castle, with three towers, dating from the Frankish period and reasonably well preserved, can be seen on a hill three kilometres away to the east. Nearby is the Byzantine church of Our Lady 'Evangelistria'.

The man-made **Lake Ladonas** lies about twelve and a half kilometres from Stavrodromi. The dam at the spot called Pidima has a height of 55 metres, and a length of 104 metres, while the lake is approximately 15 kilometres long and covers an area of 1,500 acres.

It is ideal for boating and fishing, while the surrounding hills are excellent for hunting.

An ancient myth connected with the area related how Syrinx, a nymph, ran through it escaping from the love-crazed Pan. Exhausted, she fell by the side of the river Ladon and begged the god of the river to save her. This he did, feeling sorry for her, and when Pan arrived the nymph had been turned into a reed. Pan heard the musical whistling of the wind in the reeds, cut some, tied them together, and thus made his Pan-pipes, which were called 'syrinx' in ancient times in honour of the nymph.

Near the Ladonas bridge, about 96 kilometres from Tripoli, **Loutra Iraeas** has sulphur springs which are said to be efficacious in the treatment of arthritis and rheumatism. A particularly fine mosaic was found near the remains of what is probably an ancient bath-house. The area is also known as **Liodora**.

The ruins of **Ancient Iraea**, which was built by Iraeus, the inevitable son of Lycaon, lie to the south, on the bank of the Alpheus near **Ayios Ioannis**. The city was famous for the athlete Damaretos, who won the armed race in the Olympic Games. It had two temples of Dionysus and a building for orgies, and a rather peculiar ancient tradition says that Ieraean wine had the property of making women pregnant.

ACHAÏA

Its original name was Aigialos or Aigialeia, but then, around 2000 BC, the Achaens came down from the north, they gave it their name: Achaia.

The Gulf of Patra and the Gulf of Corinth wash the shores around Araxos, Aigio and Patra. Tall mountains —Chelmos (2,355m) and Erymanthos (2,224m)— tower over the 3,271 square kilometres of the Prefecture today. The climate is cool and there is frequent rain, and the area is crossed by numerous rivers: the Pyrros, the Glafkos, the Selinoundas and the Vouraikos. Up in the mountains, at Kalavrita, a unique —for Greece— means of transport, the funicular railway, carries visitors through a landscape of unparalleled natural beauty.

The combination of natural beauty in the mountains and down by the sea with the modern development of the Prefecture distinguishes it from the rest of the Peloponnese and from much of Greece. It contains important traffic intersections and large towns as well as major tourist centres. Ferries running from Rio link the Peloponnese to Central Greece. while the harbour of Patra is the western gateway to Greece, welcoming many hundreds of visitors each day from Italy and the rest of Europe.

It was in southern Italy, at Sybaris and Kroton, that ancient Achaea had two of its most important colonies. Even in antiquity it was an economic and cultural centre of great importance. When the Macedonian dynasty began to go into decline, Achaea gave its name to an alliance of 12 cities, the Achaean League, in a vain attempt to prevent Roman penetration into Greece. After that, the area's fate was the same as that of the rest of the Peloponnese, until the arrival of the 'Franks', who made it the centre of the Principality of the Morea (or of Achaea). This led to renewed prosperity, and when the

War of Independence broke out in 1821 Achaia was a flourishing financial and commercial centre.

One of the most important occupations of the inhabitants at this time was the breeding of silk-worms and the making of silk. The silkworms were bred in the gorges of the Vouraikos river, and Kalavrita was the centre of the industry as a whole. Kalavryta and Vostistza were also known for their cheese, which was widely exported, and which they had been making since ancient times. But readers should not search for Vostitza on the map today; they will not

117

The most sacred place in the Monastery of Mega Spilaio.

find it. The town, whose name came from a type of grape which was grown in red, white and Muscat varieties, is now called Aigio. Aigio, whatever its name, has always been important as a harbour. Goods passed through it on their way to and from the whole of the Peloponnese: cheese, currants, unworked leather, cattle from the nearer islands, wine, sardines and much more. These goods were often shipped first to Patra and then on to Italy and further west.

As the area developed, important Christian centres began to appear. The monasteries of Mega Spilaio and Agia Lavra, which for centuries had been bastions of the Orthodox faith, gathered priceless treasures of Christianity and art. And it was in the courtyard of the Agia Lavra monastery that the Greeks declared the outbreak of the War of Independence of 1821, on 25 March of that year. The Achaians were in the

forefront of that war, as they were of later conflicts, including the Second Wold War and the German Occupation. Their self-sacrifices were often heroic, as in the case of the wholesale destruction of Kalavrita and the killing of the entire male population by the Occupation forces in retaliation for resistance activities.

However, the inhabitants of Achaia have always combined their national struggles with the cause of developing their own area. Today, the Prefecture hassome 275,000 inhabitants and it is the most densely populated area in the Peloponnese. Patra, the capital, is Greece's fourth largest city, and it is a centre of the greatest importance for the economy, culture and tourism. Apart from the traditional farming and fishing occupations, the Achaians today have considerable achievements in industry to boast ofQ there are textile mills, paper mills, car tyre factories and —most important of all— wineries. Achaia, and in particular the area around Patra itself, has a fine tradition in the making of wines, and the reputation of the local brands is beginning to spread outside Greece, too.

The famous Patra Carnival is a combination of high spirits, dancing, song and good wine which attracts many thousands of Greek and foreign visitors each year. And in this city with its Venetian-influenced architecture, its streets lined with neo-Classical houses, its pavements under the arches so typical of the local style, its spacious squares and its outstanding Municipal Theatre, the Carnival is supplemented on warm summer evenings by a Festival of the Arts which is gaining international recognition.

24. Diakofto - Kalavryta
(37 kms)

As we mentioned in the indroduction on the Prefecture of Achaïa, there are two roads by which Patra can be reached. One is the fast Corinth-Patra road, which does not have exits to all the seaside locations, and the other is more minor, but more picturesque and passes through all the places worth visiting along the coast. If we follow the minor coast road, after Derveni (see p. 57), we come upon the first village in Achaïa, **Aigeira**.

Remains of **Ancient Aigeira** have been found at Paliokastro and Mavra

The funicular railway runs through the Vouraikos gorge.

Litharia. Pausanias describes the ancient city as full of grand monuments and works of art.

The coast road continues north west, and, 65 kilometres from Corinth, we reach **Paralia Akratas**.

The coast road continues towards Patra, with a fascinating interplay between sea and mountain scenery. We cross the river Krathis, which is fed from the Styx spring, by whose waters the Olympian gods swore oaths.

Nearby are the resort villages of **Platanos** and **Paralia Platanou**, both popular with Greek and foreign holiday-makers.

South of **Platanos** is **Diakofto** and 2 kilometres futher on the famous Vouraïkos gorge, extending to Kalavryta, begins. There are two ways of enjoying this unique route — road and railway, the latter being the more memorable.

Thus, to the west of Platanos a road leads north west up the slopes of Mt Chelmos, through fine scenery, to **Ano Diakofto, Katholiko, Kastro, Zachlorou** and then on to the Megalo Spilaio Monastery and Kalavryta.

Diakofto, a large village with considerable commercial importance, is the starting-point for a rack-and-pinion railway up the mountain. The trip by train is memorable for its wild beauty, as the carriages wind up through the valley of the river Vouraïkos, the waters of which boil through the gorge beneath. The mountainside, alternately rocky and pineclad, rises on each side as the train climbs steep gradients and traverses bridges and tunnels.

The miraculous icon of Our Lady.

The village of **Zachlorou** (divided into Ano-Upper and Kato-Lower -Zachlorou) lies 12 kilometres from Diakofto, and is perhaps best known as a stop on the way to *the Megalo Spilaio (Great Cave) Monastery*, one of the best known in Greece. The monastery has a seven-storey building constructed across the mouth of the Chelmos cave (rebuilt in 1934, after a fire). Tradition has it that the monastery, which is dedicated to the Assumption, was founded by two monks from Thessaloniki, Theodoros and Symeon, on the spot where, in 342, Euphrosyne, a shepherd girl of royal descent, had found a miraculous icon of the Virgin in a cave with a spring. The icon is made of wax and mastich, with inlaid canvas, and is attributed to St Luke.

120

A spring a little before the Megalo Spilaio is named after the shepherdess.

The monastery once possessed many important relics and manuscripts, but most have been destroyed in successive fires. It is also known as the monastery of 'Our Lady of the Golden Cave' from its famous icon. Today Byzantine Gospels with bindings decorated with enamel and relics of saints may still be seen.

In the Middle Ages the monastery had a great deal of property in Constantinople, Smyrna and Thessaloniki, as well as large tracts of land in Achaïa and Ileia.

It enjoyed various privileges during the Turkish period, and the monks had made it a centre of learning, and when the War of Independence broke out, try as they might, the Turks could not take it.

A steep path leads to the top of the cliff, where there are the ruins of a tower and some cannon. A hostel is open for visitors. The views all around are superb.

Megalo Spilaio is a starting-point for the ascent of Mt Chelmos, a difficult climb but one which will reward the persevering with unforgettable views.

From Solo, at 990 metres, the climber can see the Waters of the Styx as they pour over a cataract ahead of him, and can continue to the head of the waterfall (Mavroneri) along the side of the wild gorge. The gorge is full of green, black and violet rocks rent asunder by some violent upheaval of the earth, and the water flows black at the bottom of the gorge, as if springing from the bowels of the earth. The water runs into the river Krathis, which in turn flows into the sea near Akrata.

On the other side are the two peaks of Mt Chelmos, snow-capped summer and winter. The water running off these peaks falls from a height of 60-70 metres on to a granite rock, with a fearful noise. These are the Waters of the Styx, today known as Mavroneri or 'Immortal Water'.

The spring of the Styx, was believed by the ancients, that be linked with another under the earth spring, whose waters flowed around Tartarus, a place in Hades where evildoers were tormented after death.

Of these waters even the Olympian gods were wary and they swore on them their most terrible oaths. Breach of any of these oaths would lead to the god being punished by a year's deep death-like sleep, and, by nine years' exclusion for that time from the councils and feasts.

These are the waters in which Thetis baptised her son Achilles, making him impossible to wound, except for the heel, by which she held him when dipping him in.

Kalavryta, whose population was massacred during the Second World War.

The railway continues from Zachlorou through more hospitable country to **Kalavryta**. The town stands at 756 metres, and has a pleasant climate, being cool in the summer, and a fine situation. It stands on the site of ancient **Cynaetha**, on a plain at the foothills of Mt Chelmos. The name the town bears today dates from the Middle Ages, and derives from the words 'kala vryta', meaning good springs. There are plenty of springs still, inside and outside the town: Kalavrytini, Findayi, Keramidaki, Souleimani, Vrysoula, Tzami, Gerizomana, Alimbei, Tria Pigadia etc.

One of them, Kalavrytini, is identified with the ancient spring of Alyssus (Pausanias says that it was under a plane tree and that its waters cured rabies and other illnesses, as well as countering the evil influences of the Styx). Cynaetha underwent repeated destruction through the centuries. In the Middle Ages it was the seat of a baron, with 12 fiefs.

The area around Kalavryta is interesting from many points of view for naturalists, tourists, historians and archaeologists. About an hour to the east, on a cliff at a height of 1,190 metres, is the castle built by the De Tournai barons to guard the Chelmos passes. The Turks in the castle were besieged by the Greeks on 21 March 1821, and the first cannon shots were

fired from a spot opposite, where an old cannon stands today.

The castle is popularly known as the 'Kastro tis Oraias' (Castle of the Beautiful Girl), from the legend of a beautiful Palaeologue princess, daughter of the baron of Halandritsa, who jumped from the walls rather than fall into the hands of the Turks.

The historic monastery of Ayia Lavra stands on an impressive hill 7 kilometres to the south west of Kalavryta. (In Byzantine times, a 'lavra' was a group of cells for hermits).

It was founded by a monk from Mount Athos in 961, about 300 metres to the east of the present posi-

Above, the historic church of the Old Monastery of Ayia Lavra; below, the Monastery with the Memorial in the background.

*The banner
of the War of Independence (1821).*

Climbers and skiers interested in Mt Chelmos may also start from Kalavryta. There is a shelter at Diaselo, four hours away at an altitude of 2,100 metres, and this is one of the best organised in Greece. The shelter can be reached even more easily (in about 2½ hours) from Peristera, 27 kilometres from Akrata.

The road which leads south from Kalavryta towards Tripoli makes possible visits to many of the attractive villages of the Kalavryta province.

In the village of **Plataniotissa** there is a strange chapel, dedicated to the Virgin, constructed in the hollow of an ancient plane tree.

Well worth a visit in the **Kastria** area is an imposing cave, of great scientific interest. Inside there are 15 lakes, divided by unusual natural dams and spectacular cataracts.

tion. The monastery was destroyed three times over. The banner of the Greek Revolution, raised here on 18 March, 1821, is still to be seen, with a hole in it made by a Turkish bullet.

There are fine wall-paintings in the church of St Nicholas (Franco Catanello, 16th century) and at Palaiomonastiro (notably a Crucifixion of 1645).

In the Museum are, among other things, a Gospel studded with diamonds, a gift of Catherine the Great, the skull of St Alexios, and the crozier and vestments of Bishop Yermanos.

There are two roads leading west out of Kalavryta; one of these continues west to Patra (we shall follow its course below), while the other goes south to Tripoli (in Arcadia, see p. 112).

On the latter road lie the villages of **Longovouni**, **Priolithos** and **Kato Kleitoria**, with ruins of ancient Cleitor.

25. Kalavryta - Tripoli
(91 kms)

South of Kalavryta and 11 kms to the south of Kleitoria, there is a branch off the road to the west and the villages of **Dafni** and **Tripotama**, while the main road continues further south, leading to Tripoli (see p. 112).

The attractive town of **Dafni**, in a natural green amphitheatre above the Vertsiotiko river, is renowned for its dry and healthy climate and is a well-known summer resort. It has a number of Byzantine churches and the surrounding countryside is ideal for exploration and walks.

A little way outside Dafni is the Byzantine Monastery of the Annunciation, on a site with many plane trees.

Also extremely attractive are **Mana**, about 2 kms from Dafni, well-watered and with tall plane trees, and **Kakatsova**, at 5 kms, with its mountain scenery.

To the south west and at a distance of some 46 kms from Kalavryta, the village of **Tripotama** stands at a height of 550 m. The name of the town ('three rivers') comes from the fact that it stands at the confluence of the Seiraios (Vertsiotiko), the Aroanios (Livardzino) and the Erymanthos (Nousaitiko) rivers. Their meeting-point coincides with the Achaïa, Ileia and Arcadia boundaries. Further to the west, the road goes to Patra and Amaliada.

Another well-known resort that attracts many summer visitors is the village of **Livartzi**, which stands on the edge of a valley formed by the river of that name, at a height of 800 m. It is surrounded by the slopes of Mt Erymanthos; its little square has enormous plane trees and an abundant spring.

26. Kalavryta - Patra
(74 kms)

The road to Patra lies to the west of Kalavryta; the first village reached on this road, at 15 kms, is verdant **Flamboura**.

At approximately 28 kilometres is the village of **Kato Vlasia** and, near it, the summer resort of **Micha**. There are two monasteries nearby — of St John the Baptist and of St Nicholas.

The main road continues, passing through the villages of **Platanos, Kalanos** and **Kalanistra**.

Nearby, above the gorge, is the Monastery of the Nativity of Our Lady "Chrysopodaritissa' and the village of **Chrysopighi**.

At 42 kilometres a minor road off to the right (north) climbs to the villages of **Demesticha** (it stands in a small fertile plain whose grapes produce the well-known wine named after the place) and **Leontio** (Gourzoumissa).

Among the ruins of the small ancient city of Leontion, a small elegant theatre of the 4th century BC is particularly attractive.

The town of **Halandritsa** lies at a distance of some 55 kilometres from Kalavryta. Here there are the ruins of a medieval castle, a reminder that in 1209 the town was nominated by the Franks as the seat of a barony.

A minor road to the south brings us to the charming villages of **Elliniko** (at 500 metres), **Koumari** (at 900 metres) and **Kalousi** (at 750 metres) on the thickly-wooded slopes of Mt Erymanthos.

From Halandritsa the road continues north west and arrives at the fork of 'Skorda to Hani' ('The Garlic-seller's Inn'); from there it passes through **Ovria** and finally comes to Patra — the western gateway to Greece.

Egeo: the upper town, called 'Psila Alonia'.

27. Diakofto - Aiyion - Patra (55 kms)

After Diakofto (see p. 119), the coast road gradually ceases to be a coast road.

At about the 87th kilometre we enter **Eliki**, which the visitor would be tempted to identify with the ancient city of Helike, which was capital of the Achaean League. The ruins of the ancient city, however, lie some 30-40 metres under the surface of the sea, at the mouth of the river Selinous, as they have done since the city's destruction by earthquake in 373 BC.

Near **Temeni**, before the bridge over the river Selinous, a side road to the left climbs south up to **Selinous**, which stands among dense greenery and deep gorges, **Achladia**, which

stands on a hill, **Lakka** and **Fteri**. Fteri is a well-known resort which has a pine forest, at 1,150 metres, and just outside the village is a natural platform known locally as 'God's Balcony', which has a wonderful view over the Gulf of Corinth.

The main road turns north, crosses the Selinous bridge and enters Aiyio.

Aiyio is the second largest and second most important town of Achaïa, and is an important commercial and industrial centre.

In some versions of the mythology, it was here that Agamemnon called together the Greek leaders to decide on the Trojan expedition. It was one of the cities in the Achaean League and became its capital after the destruction of Helike. The League had a temple here, to Homarian Zeus, in which the representatives of

127

the cities held their meetings. All that remains of the ancient city are some walls on the hill above the harbour and an underground passage carved out of the rock, with store-rooms and cisterns.

It then went through the hands of various tyrants before passing to the Romans in 146. In 23 AD it was destroyed by a fearful earthquake, and attempts to put it back on its feet lasted right through Byzantine times.

The town was renamed Vostitsa by the Slavs who conquered it in the 8th century, and it bore this name until its eventual liberation from the Turks. In 1209 it was the seat of a Frankish barony, and in 1422 was taken by the Palaeologue family, only to be surrendered to the Turks in 1458.

The interior of the cathedral and, below, Egeo harbour.

The church of Our Lady 'Trypiti', hewn out of the rock.

A fine view across the Gulf of Corinth to the mountains of Central Greece may be had from Psila Alonia, in the Upper Town.

The springs of Aiyio were known in antiquity. Among the churches, that of the Dormition of the Virgin ('Faneromeni'), a 13th century cathedral with a fine screen, the Archangels (17th century) and St Andrew (18th century) are of special interest. Near the town is the unusual church of Our Lady 'Tripiti', built in the hollow of a rock.

The church has a miraculous icon covered with votive offerings and a great feast is held there on the Friday after Easter. There are also celebrations in the town in May, with dances, parades, etc.

A road south from Aiyio leads through **Kato Mouriki** and **Ayios Ioannis**, before reaching, near **Kouninas** (600 metres), the Monastery of the Archangels, on a fine site in the foothills of Mt Klokos. This was first built by the Palaeologue family of Mystras at the near by site of Paliomonastiro in the early 15th century, and was dedicated to the Blessed Leontios of Monemvasia, who lived as an anchorite not far away. After fires in 1621 and 1628, the monastery was rebuilt on its present site. During the Revolution it was a centre of activity and was burned by the Turks.

The monastery today has a museum with fine Byzantine and post-Byzantine icons, historical documents, illuminated gospels, reliquaries, the vestments of Patriarch Gregory V and other vestments, embroidered church hangings, and a

129

The attractive little fishing village of Psathopyrgos.

library of some 4,000 books. There is a nunnery ('Pepelenitsa') at Stavros nearby.

The coast road passes through the area known as **Lambiri**, which is becoming internationally known as a tourist centre. Every summer visitors drawn by the area's combination of pine woods and beaches use the camping facilities available to create a whole happy community of holiday-makers.

There are tourist facilities all along the road, with a Club Méditerranée camp and an organised beach at **Longos**.

The main road continues along the shores of a small bay before entering the pretty fishing village of **Psathopyrgos**.

At 127 kilometres from Corinth, in

the village of **Ayios Yeorgios**, there is a turning right (north) to **Rio**. From here it is only a short ferry trip to **Antirio**, on the shores of Central Greece. The crossing takes about 15 minutes. Rio preserves remains of a Venetian castle known as the Castle of the Morea or Kastelli.

Seven kilometres to the south west of Rio lies Patra, the largest city in the Peloponnese.

The town as seen from its medieval castle.

Patra

Patra is one of the most important provincial towns in Greece, and can be regarded as the country's western gate, since there is a great deal of passenger and commercial traffic by sea between here and Italy.

The town is a very ancient one, having been founded during the Late Mycenean period. Ionian colonists from Attica appeared around 1400 BC, setting up three agricultural communities —Antheia, Mesatis and Aroe. In the 11th century B.C.

The church of St Andrew, patron saint of the town, symbol of Patra.

Patra: Ayiou Yeorgiou Square.

Achaeans from Laconia moved in, after being thrown out of their own region by the Dorians, and the area took their name, while Patreus, their leader, gave his to the city which resulted from the amalgamation of the earlier cities.

Patra allied itself with Athens and Argos, thus competing with Corinth. St Andrew brought the message of Christianity to Patra, only to be crucified here. He is the town's patron saint and his imposing church stands on the sea-front. The town flourished during the Byzantine period. The modern town was built on the site of the ancient city by Ioannis Capodistrias, first Governor of free Greece.

The town has two parts — the Upper and the Lower. The Upper Town stands on a hill known as Psila Alonia, has a fine view, and to the north east is a hill on which stand the remains of the Venetian castle, on the site of the ancient acropolis, where there was a temple of Panachaean Athena and a senetuary to Laphrian Artemis. Next to Ayiou Yeorgiou Sq., on the slopes of this hill, is a Roman Odeion, which has been reconstructed, and a Roman aqueduct. A little further up are the Byzantine-style churches of the Pantokrator and Pantanassa (which has a fine belfry and rich decoration). The town museum, facing Olgas Sq., has a collection of important archaeological finds.

The Patra Carnival, which takes just before the beginning of Lent, is internationally famous, with its dancing and parades of decorated floats and masked revellers. In recent years a summer festival has become established, with musical, theatrical and other cultural events.

Near the city, in a beautiful situation, is the old Byzantine 'Yerokomeio' Monastery — it lies 2 kilometres from the town.

If we take a minor road out of Patra to the north east, through groves of orange, lemon, pear and peach trees, we come, after 3 kilometres to a fork to the right (south west).

This fork will lead us to to Achaïa-Clauss wine production unit, in an impressive position overlooking the Gulf of Patra. Tours of the factory are available, and the laboratories and the famous vaults may be visited. The wine may be tasted in a special lounge where autographs of famous personalities (scientists, artists and politicians) who have visited the factory are on display.

About 1 kilometre after the turning for the Achaïa-Clauss factory, the road reaches the Glafkos hydroelectric station. The artificial lake which feeds the station is at **Souli**, a short distance away.

The two mountain shelters on Mt Panachaikon are reached by a minor road leading east out of Patra.

Patra harbour, the gateway to western Greece.

28. Patra - Pyrgos
(98 kms)

The old Patra-Pyrgos road leaves Patra to the south west through a rather unprepossessing industrial area. We then come to **Itia**, where there are organised tourist facilities, and **Mintilogli**, another popular bathing spot.

There is a cave with stalactites and stalagmites near the village of **Portes**.

A short distance further on to the south west near Riolo, there is a spring known as 'the gunpowder spring' (baroutovrysi) from the smell of its waters, which is reputedly beneficial in the treatment of rheumatism.

We cross the river Peiros and after two kilometres enter **Kato Achaïa**, built on the site of ancient **Dyme**.

This was the most westerly of the Achaean cities, and was also known as Paleia, Stratos and Caukones. Supposedly founded by the Epeians, early inhabitants of the Peloponnese, it had a temple and statue of Athena and a sanctuary of the Twin Mother (Rhea-Cybele), as well as one of Attis. After 756 BC it was united with nearby **Olenos** — which lay to the north east of Kato Achaïa and of which ruins have been found and other cities. Freed of the Macedonians in the 3rd century, it constituted part of the Achaean League in 281-280, but was forced to accept a Macedonian garrison in the reign of Philip V.

It opposed Roman rule, and indeed revolted against it, in 120-115. The town was occupied, however, and Pompey colonised it with pirates from Cilicia in Asia Minor, which proved an unsuccessful experiment. After this Augustus incorporated it into the administrative unit run from Patra. Some ruins of Dyme can be seen near **Lakkopetra**.

West of Kato Achaïa, the road passes through **Paralimni** (Araxos) and **Mavron Oros** before ending at Cape Araxos. There is a thermal spring between Lakkopetra and Paralimni which smells of sulphur and is, as usual, reputed to be efficacious in the cure of almost anything. To the east of the road between Paralimni and the Cape is a shallow lagoon, which the local inhabitants use for fish-farming. The military aerodrome at Araxos is occasionally used for civilian flights.

After Kato Achaïa the road turns south west, with small picturesque villages to the left and right. We enter **Sageïka**, where a turning to the left (south) leads to **Yerouseïka, Tsakonika** and **Riolo.**

Lapas, thirty five kilometres along the road from Patra, is the site of the Pelasgian city of **Larisa**, on the banks of the Larisos river.

The Pyrgos road continues to the south of Lapas, crossing the Vergas bridge and entering Elia (see p. 139).

29. Patra - Elia (58 kms)

A road which leaves Patra to the south comes after approximately 8 kilometres to **Orvia**, where there is a turning for **Mintilogli** and its fine beach and thence on to the Patra-Pyrgos road.

At 10 kilometres the main road forks, at the 'Skorda to Hani'. The branch to the South East leads to Kalavryta (see p. 126) and from there to Tripoli. The road to the south goes to the villages of **Vasiliko, Starochori** and **Hiona**, entering the Elia region.

At 18 kilometres from Patra, the branch of the road to the right (west) leads to the picturesque villages of **Petsakitika, Isoma, Chaikali, Peristera** and **Theriano** before joining the main Patra-Pyrgos road.

Between Petsakitina and Isoma yet another minor road runs southwest to **Fares**, (altitude 120 metres) reputed to be the site of ancient **Pharae**.

This was one of the oldest Achaean cities —built in the myths, by Pharis, son of Philodameia and grandson of Danaos— and later joined the Achaean League. It was relieved of Macedonian control and joined the new Achaean League (278-274 B.C.). It was sacked by the Aetolians, but Pausanias mentions that in his time part of the Agora was still visible, as was the marble statue of Agoraios Hermes, with a famous oracle. Under Augustus Caesar the city came under the jurisdiction of the commander of Patra.

The main road continues south from the 18 kilometre fork, with turnings to the right and left for **Erymantheia, Greveno** (1,550 metres with the ruins of a castle which played an important role in the last years of Turkish occupation), **Velimachi** (in Arcadia) and **Kalentzi**, at 975 metres, with thick pine woods and a marvellous view over the plain to Cephalonia and Zakynthos (Zante). The route to the summit of Mt Erymanthos (2,254 metres) begins here.

At **Panouseika** there is a thermal spring suitable for cases of rheumatism. To the west are **Ayia Varvara** and **Kalfas**, in a deep gorge filled with pine trees. The Kalfeiko river which runs through the gorge is the boundary between Achaïa and Elia.

From **Skiadas** (350 m) the Notenon Monastery can be reached in about one hour's walk. A little further up there is a cave which was used as a hiding place by Greeks escaping from the Turkish authorities. There is ample opportunity for hunting in the area.

To the north west we come to **Skouras** (270 metres), after which the bridge at **Mylos Karpeta** again marks the Achaïa-Elia border.

To the south of Ayia Triada the road forks: the branch which goes to the west leads to Amaliada (see p. 143), while that to the east is for Tripoli (see p. 112).

ELIA

The site of Ancient Olympia is sacred; this is the land of the Olympic Games, of the ancient and eternal Olympic Spirit. Here, at one of the most important and official sanctuaries in Greece, the myths say that Heracles founded the Olympic Games. In the 8th century BC, Iphitus reorganished them, and for the first time instituted the the Olympic truce: that is, while the Games were in progress military clashes throughout Greece came to a standstill. In this way, Olympism became a symbol of peace.

The ancient Olympic Games lasted five days. Only men and boys were permitted to take part in the events, which includedfoot races, the pentathlon, wrestling, boxing, the pancrateion (a from of all-in wrestling), chariot races and foot races for men in full armour. The Games were so important to the ancient Greeks that they began their system of chronology from the date of the first Games.

In the calm, green valley of Olympia, surrounded by low hills , we can still walk through the wild olive trees towards the temples of Olympian Zeus and Hera, and as we walk across the magnificent Stadium it is possible to feel that the Olympic spirit really has lived on. For the Olympic Games were never merely a sporting contest: the participants came to be purified, to be contestants in a competition so innocent of profit that the only prize for victors was a wreath of wild olive and the knowledge that they had won.

The natural environment must have played an important part in making the Games what they became. Nature here, in the seemingly endless valley of the Alpheios as it runs down to the Ionian, breathes peace. The winter is mild, and the summer warm and dry; the frequent rains fill up the two large rivers, the Pineios and the Alpheios.

Map of the Prefecture of Ileia

There are lakes at Agoulinitsa, Mouria, and Kaiafa, where the mineral springs are famous. The river Anigros has its estuary nearby. The water of this river contains sulphur, and it was known even in ancient times for its medicinal properties. The only trouble was its unpleasant smell, which accounts for its name: 'anigros' means dirty, base, evil, foul-smelling. The myth to account for this state of affairs was that the Lernaean Hydra, which lived nearby, had poured its poison into the river.Here, then, it was that Heracles fought with this mythical beast and killed it.

In the Homeric poems, the inhabitants of the area were called Epeioi and Pylioi, and they were descended from a mixture of Phoenicians, Aeolians of Thessaly, Leleges, Pelasgians and Caucones from Arcadia. These people formed three small states: Coile Elis, Pisatis and Triphylia. When the Dorians arrived and conquered the Peloponnese, the Eleians were forced to ally themselves with Sparta. This cost them heavily in the Peloponnesian War, when they had to fight the forces of Athens and Corcyra (Corfu) They were later conquered by the Macedonians. The area formed part of the Achaean League and came under Roman domination at an early date.

Eleia ceased to be a centre of importance throughout the Greek world when the Byzantine Emperor Theodosius banned the Olympic Games in 393 AD. In the centuries which followed, it suffered the fate of the rest of the Peloponnese, being invaded by Goths, Avars, Saracens, Bulgarians, Normans and Franks. In 1430, the area was taken by Constantine Palaiologos, but in 1460 it finally bowed to Turkish rule. The Turks stayed until ultimate liberation in 1828, with a brief interval of Venetian conquest in 1687-1715.

There can be no doubt that the fertility of this part of the Peloponnese was always a factor which attracted prospective conquerors.

The Prefecture has a total area of 2,617 square kilometres, most of it lying in the plain of Eleia, where the Alpheios river, the largest in the Peloponnese, flows into the sea. The area has alwsys been known for its fine farmland:

"All the countryside around, as far as Glarentza, is planted with wheat, maize and other cereals. The local people make large quantities of cheese from sheep's milk and they breed silkworms whose cocoons are much finer than those of Kalamata. Cotton can also be grown in these parts" (Pouqueville).

With the exception of the silkworms, the other agricultural occupations of the Eleians have not changed down to the present. They also grow grapes, sweet watermelons, melons and the full range of citrus fruits, not to mention potatoes. There are pistachio trees, too, which grow in the sandy soil next to the long golden beaches of the Ionian Sea. Those beaches, with their superb sunsets, are now lined with tourist resorts whose up-to-date facilities are a major source of income for the local people.

The fertility of the soil and the development of tourism have managed to keep a population of some 160,000 almost unchanged, although many local people have moved to Athens and elsewhere in search of a better future.

30. Patra - Gastouni
(67 kms)

The old road enters the western extremity of Achaia (see p. 134) and runs down into the fertile Eleian plain, the largest in the Peloponnese.

A minor road leads north west from **Varda**. Nearby is the town of **Manolada**, built by the Franks in the Middle Ages.

Manolada today is a sizeable commercial and agricultural centre, known for its water-melons, cheese and sheep's yoghurt. There is a small but attractive wood of oak trees, which was once a sizeable forest. Nearby is the pretty church of 'Palaiopanayia'.

The road continues to the north, from Manolada, coming to **Loutra Kounoupeliou** or Irminis whose water is used in the treatment of rheumatism. The surrounding area is most attractive, with pine woods, clean beaches and a sparkling sea.

The Homeric city of **Hyrmine** was sited on this spot. According to the myths Hyrmine was founded by Actor, husband of Molione, sister of Augeus, king of Epeieia. The remains of Pelasgian walls can still be seen near the baths, while a nearby hill has ruins of a Frankish castle on its peak and of a medieval church of St Peter at its foot.

South west of Varda we reach **Lechaina**, 62 kilometres from Patra, a town which is known to have existed before the 14th century. It is men-

tioned (as Lechaino or Leichaina) in documents of 1324 as belonging to John of Granine, Prince of Achaïa. It seems that the town was first built on the coast, but attacks by pirates in Turkish times made it imperative for a safer site inland to be found.

Nowadays, it is an agricultural and commercial centre for the surrounding fertile area, and its main claim to fame is as the birthplace of the 19th century writer Andreas Karkavitsas, whose bust stands in the main square.

At some 3 kilometres from Lechaina, on the Spiliadis estate, there is a medicinal spring whose waters are reputed to be beneficial as a laxative and for neuralgic and skin complaints.

Minor roads lead to Kotychi lake (where wild duck may be hunted), **Alykes, Myrsini, Kyllini** and its baths.

Kyllini is to the west of Lechaina on the site of ancient **Cyllene** and the medieval city of Glarentza (Clarence).

The **ancient Killini** was the port of Elis, and was founded by Arcadians from the area of Mt Zireia. The Arcadians brought the worship of Hermes to the coast, as well as that of Asclepius and Aphrodite.

The medieval city, known by a number of variants of its name, was built between 1210 and 1218 by Geoffrey I Villehardouin, who was also responsible for the castle of Chlemoutsi, later to be known as Castel Tornese from the mint which operated there and produced coins called 'tornese'.

The village of **Kastro** stands above Kyllini, and towering over the last houses of the village are the imposing ruins of the Villehardouin fort, generally regarded as the best and most representative example of Frankish military architecture in the Peloponnese. The outer walls are in good condition, despite the hole that Ibrahim blew in them in 1823.

A plaque over the entrance commemorates Constantine Palaeologus' stay in the castle. The size and magnificence of the chambers gives some idea of the life led in it by its first inhabitants, and its topmost battlements afford a wonderful view over the Ionian Islands and the Peloponnese.

Loutra Kyllinis, the baths, are

The popular camp site at Loutra Kyllinis, and Arkoudi with its narrow alleys.

nearby to the south in a eucalyptus wood. Its seven springs were well-known in ancient times, and are considered especially good for afflictions of the respiratory system. The remains of Roman baths have been found nearby.

South of Lechaina, the main road continues and enters **Andravida**, a commercial and agricultural centre

known world-wide for the horses it breeds. There was a medieval town of the same name here, and, in the 13th century, it was one of the most important in Elia. The Franks called it Andreville, and made it the capital of the principality of the Morea and the seat of a Catholic bishop.

The Gothic church of St Sophia still survives, in part. This was the bishop's cathedral until the 15th century. The Kourti, or Frankish parliament, met in Andravida, and there were spectacular races amongst mounted knights. Three Villehardouin princes ruled the town and died there before the collapse of Frankish influence.

The main road continues south west and, after about 70 kilometres from Patra, enters **Kavasila**, another agricultural town with a considerable production of currants.

There is a local railway to Vartholomio and Kyllini (Loutra).

Just past Kavasila we cross the river Pineios and enter **Gastouni**, an agricultural and commercial centre where again there is much horse-breeding. The plain of Gastouni, watered by the Pineios, is one of the most fertile in Greece.

The site of today's town was occupied by a Byzantine city before the 10th century, as can be seen from the fact that the Byzantine Church of the Dormition has an inscription stating that it was renovated in 1072. During the period of Turkish rule, Gastouni was the capital of Elia, and had special privileges. During the War of Independence, it served as a supply centre for the Greek forces, but when the country was liberated the town went into decline.

Every May a flower festival is held here, with parades of floats and other events.

A road leaving Gastouni to the east leads to **Ancient Elis** and the artificial lake of Pineios.

Ancient Elis, dating back to prehistoric times, lay between the modern villages of Avyeio, Kalyvia, Nea Ilida and Ilida. The town was rich, and famous for its role in the supervision of the Olympic Games. The age of the site is shown by the discovery of Mycenean tombs.

Excavations on the site have brought to light one of the largest Greek theatres yet found, the agora, the acropolis, the gymnasium, the palaestra and other buildings. Vessels, copper 'tickets' and various pieces of jewellery have been found in the theatre.

The artificial Pineios lake is near the ancient site.

Another road brings us (west) to **Vartholomio**, supposedly named after a Frankish knight, Bartholomew, who wooed and won a beautiful Greek girl called Lygia. The village was the scene of heroic resistance to Ibrahim Pasha in 1825, when 200 men of the village fought superior forces and were all killed.

From Vartholomio the road continues westwards to Loutra Kyllinis, while another road leads north to **Neochori**.

30. Amaliada - Pyrgos
(20 kms)

From Gastouni the main road turns to the south east and at a distance of approximately 10 kilometres enters **Amaliada**, a major urban centre of this fertile region, which produces currants, olive oil, potatoes and citrus fruit. The town is new, its name deriving from Queen Amalia (19th century), and perhaps its only point of interest to the tourist is the games held here every May in commemoration of Koroivos, first Elian Olympic victor. Concerts, theatrical performances and other celebrations take place at the same time.

However, the spot known as **Frankavila**, with its Byzantine church, 2 kilometres from the town, is worth visiting.

Thirteen kilometres from here, an a hill, is the monastery of St Nicholas ('of the Frank's jump').

The name stems from a tradition that some Frankish knight, to avoid his pursuers, said a prayer to St Nicholas and jumped off the top of the hill on his horse, without either of them being injured in the slightest.

A road leaves Amaliada to the north east and passing through Havari, Efyra and Simopoulo, forks at Ayia Triada, the branch to the north going to Patra (see p. 135) and that to the east to Tripotama and Tripoli (see p. 126).

A road to the south west from Amaliada leads to **Kourouta** (buses in the summer) where there is a fine wide beach.

We continue south towards Pyrgos. Just before the town, a minor road to the right (south west) takes us to the Katakolos region, while another soon after (north west) goes to **Lasteïka** and **Ayios Yeorgios**.

After covering a distance of 97 kilometres from Patra, we enter **Pyrgos**, a major agricultural and commercial centre, and the capital of the Prefecture of Elia. There is evidence of ancient occupation of the site — perhaps here was Dyspontion, an outpost of Pisa.

The modern town got its name (meaning 'tower') from a tower built on the Eparcheion hill by a poor villager who became a bey. This man, Yorgos Tsorotas, came down to the plain to work from the mountain village of Tserota near Kalavryta. While working in the fields, he came across treasure in the form of ancient gold coins, a large number of which he offered to the Sultan Selim I. In gratitude, the Sultan made him a gift of all the surrounding area and made him a bey. This story is placed at around the end of the 15th century or the beginning of the 16th. Some houses grew up around the tower and a town gradually developed.

When its Greek owner died without issue, the area reverted to the Sultan, who gave Pyrgos and its surroundings to the female chief of the harem, the Valide-Sultana. The town grew under the protection of the Sultan's court. In 1678, when the first Turkish commander was appointed, there were more than 5,000 inhabitants. After some years under the Venetians, the town passed back to the Turks in 1715, and was made the seat of a voivode. The local Greek

Pyrgos and the sea behind, seen from the Eparchy building.

families had made important progress economically when the Revolution came, and were thus able to supply a well-organised background for the struggle for freedom. Almost as soon as the Revolution broke out —on 29 March 1821— the local forces, led by the dignitaries of the town, chased the Turks out of the area and forced them to take refuge in the castle at Kyllini.

During the early years of the War, many men of Pyrgos fought heroically in their town area and in other parts of Greece. In 1825, however, Ibrahim Pasha had his revenge, burning the city and selling the women and children into slavery.

Pyrgos today is an attractive town with a pleasant climate. The pine-shaded Town Hall square, where the Cathedral of St Nicholas also stands, and the neighbouring Eparcheio square have fine views over the plain and the lakes of Mouria, Kasta and Agoulinitsa, where there are plentiful eels and fish and where various birds may be hunted during migratory periods. The Ionian and the mountains round Olympia may also be seen.

The town has a library of 20.000 volumes and a small art gallery with works by local painters. For many years the famous writer and poet Takis Doxas worked in the library. Pyrgos also has the Currant Institute of the Autonomous Currant Organisation, which conducts into Currants and other crops.

St Charalambos, patron of the town, is celebrated with great pomp on February 10.

A road leading north east from Pyrgos soon comes to a fork. Taking the southern branch, we pass through **Katarrachi** and arrive at **Spiatza**, an excellent clean beach close to the mouth of the river Alpheios.

A crossroads near the coast leads to **Ayios Andreas**, with a fine beach and amenities and the remains of **Ancient Pheia**, another port of ancient Elis. The acropolis of the city was on the hill known today as Pontikokastro, and both Byzantines and Franks built on the ruins of the ancient walls; the Franks called it Beauvoir.

Part of the ancient city is now covered by water, at a depth of 10 metres. The road continues to **Korakochori** and from there to Skourichori and Myrtia.

The southern branch of this crossroads goes to **Alkyona**, again with a good beach, and from there to **Katakolo**, the port of Pyrgos. The local products (chiefly currants) are exported from the small artificial harbour. Good beaches are to be found in the neighbourhood.

Of interest are the murals in the post-Byzantine church and the exhibits in the museum of the monastery.

Katakolo,
the port for Pyrgos, and its long beach.

32. Pyrgos - Olympia
(10 kms)

The main road forks in Pyrgos, and one branch out of the town goes to the east, towards Ancient Olympia. This is the road taken by all those, foreign and Greek, who wish to pay homage to the site where the ideals of the Olympic spirit were born.

The journey itself would be worth taking even if the destination were not so important; we run through a land of gardens, orchards, orange and lemon trees, flowers and vines.

Near Lanthi is the Kremasti Monastery, built about 1600 in a cave halfway up a steep cliff. It has an icon of Our Lady which is traditionally attributed to St Luke.

The Olympia road passes through **Smila**, entering the fertile Pelopian plain. The ancient city of **Herakleia** in Pisa stood between the modern village of the same name and **Pournari**. The city was a member of the Pisa group, and was famous for its medicinal springs — according to one myth, Athena sent Heracles here to bathe.

The springs were dedicated to the four daughters of the hero Ion, the Ionian Nymphs. Today, the springs are employed in the treatment of rheumatism and arthritis.

The village of **Pelopio**, 16 kilometres from Pyrgos, is almost literally smothered in lush vegetation; pines, olives, almonds, lemon and orange trees, cypresses, planes and willows abound.

In a small valley haunted by nightingales stands a fine monastery dedicated to St John, and the view over the plains, the mountains and the Ionian from the nearby Petrovouni hill is superb.

Ancient Olympia

After about 19 kilometres from Pyrgos, we enter the valley of Olympia, no less fertile and famous now than it was in ancient times. The river Kladeos, on the left, forms one boundary, with the Alpheios, to the right in a course lined with pines and olives, forming the other.

The modern village of **Ancient Olympia** is built on a sloping hillside near the fabled ruins of the ancient site. The history of the site, at least in mythology, goes back almost as far as the myths themselves: to the story of Cronus and his children.

There was a shrine and altar to Mother Earth at Olympia, with an oracle sacred to her, as wife of Uranus and mother of Cronus. When Cronus overthrew his father, say the myths, he took over this shrine and named it after himself. But he, too, was driven out by his son, Zeus, to whom the area was sacred from then on, and the oracle became his.

As for the origin of the Olympic Games, there are various traditions among which one can pick and choose. Some say that they were established by the Kouretes from Crete, others that Aethlius, first mythical king of Elis, whose name is said to have given us the word 'athlete', was responsible, while a third group put their money on Pelops. One other legend has it that

The sacred grove in the lush and well-watered plain of Olympia.

the Olympian gods themselves competed against each other at Olympia.

No matter what the answer to this may be, if, indeed, it could be said that there is one, we can be sure that the site was a centre for pilgrims from all over Greece at least as far back as the 11th century BC. In 884, Iphitus, descendant of Heracles and lord of Elis, Lycurgus, also descended from Heracles and ruler of Sparta, and Cleosthenes, king of Pisa, agreed that Olympia and the whole of Elis would be regarded as a sacred area.

They further agreed that there should be a truce throughout the country on the dates on which the Olympic Games were to take place. This agreement was inscribed in circular fashion on a bronze disc which was seen by Pausanias in the 2nd century AD.

Apart from their importance as an institution for the promotion of the brotherhood of mankind and as an example of true sportsmanship, the Games are also vital for our knowledge of the dates at which events in ancient Greece took place. The victory of the runner Coroebos in 776 is taken as the first Games and the beginning of the historical period in Greece.

In the beginning, the Games consisted of only one event, the foot-race, and they lasted only one day. Later, further events were added: foot-races of greater distance and in armour, horse and chariot races, wrestling and the Pankration, which was a kind of all-in wrestling, boxing, events for boys, and so on. By the Classical period there were 18 events and the whole festival lasted 5 days.

147

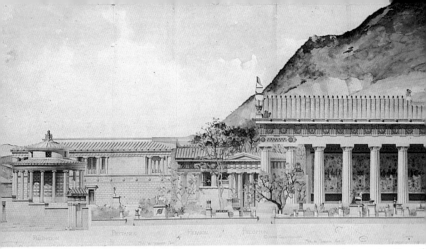

A reconstruction of

THE ARCHAEOLOGICAL SITE OF OLYMPIA

1.Entrance 2.Plain of Mars, Gymnasium 3.Palaestra 4.River Kladeos 5.Greek Baths 6.Roman House 7.Heroon 8.Roman House 9.Pheidias' Workshop 10.Leonidaion 11. Propylum 12.Southern Baths 13.Philippeion 14.Temple of Hera 15.Banqueting Hall 16.Exedra of Herod Atticus 17.To Patra and the Museum 18.Treasuries 19.Stadium Entrance 20.Stadium 21.Echo-Hall 22.Metroon 23.Prehistoric Houses 24.Pelopion 25.Theatre 26.Monument of Ptolemy II and Arsinoe 27.Base of Zeus Statue 28.Base of Dropios Statue 29.Offering of Mikythos 30.Temple of Zeus 31.Position of the Olive Tree from which the Victors were Crowned 32.Base of the Paionos Victory Statue 33.Altar 34.South East House (Hellanodikeion) 35.Roman Triumphal Arch 36.Bouleuterion 37.South Hall 38.Mt Kronio 39.To Tripoli 40.Medieval Bed of the Alpheios

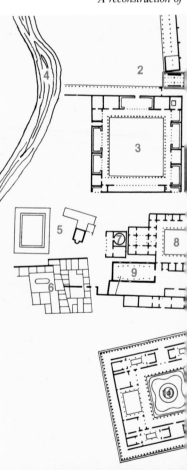

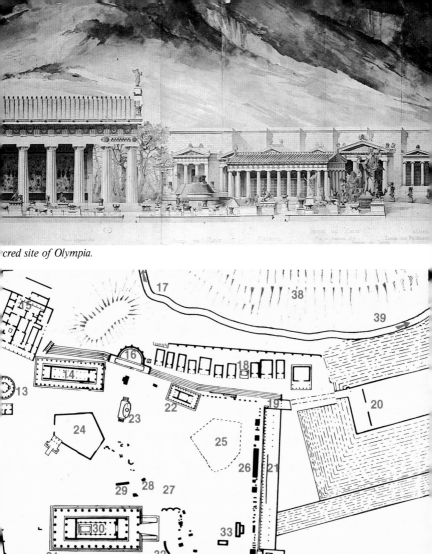

...cred site of Olympia.

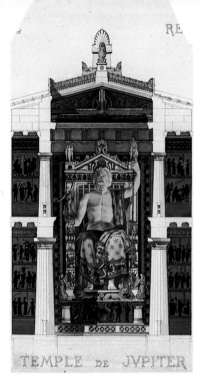

TEMPLE DE JVPITER

A reconstruction of the chryselephantine statue of Zeus, one of the seven wonders of the ancient world.

The athletes, who came from all over Greece and her colonies, did not compete in the hope of setting new records, but to win an honourable victory. Victors were crowned with the 'kotino' — a wreath made with the leaves of an ancient wild olive tree which stood outside the temple of Zeus. Anyone who won three events at the Olympics, or the same event three times, was entitled to have a statue of himself raised within the sacred precincts.

Apart from the men's and boys' Games, Pan-Hellenic Games for girls were also held every four years. They were called the Heraean Games, after the goddess Hera, who was also worshipped in the locality.

Although the Olympic Games had begun to lose something of their brilliance even as far back as the 4th century BC, they were not finally abolished until the Byzantine Emperor Theodosius I did away with them in 393 AD. After that, the site on which the Games had been held was neglected, and many of the buildings and statues were flattened by terrible earthquakes in the third decade of the sixth century. Rain over the centuries brought earth down from Kronion hill, gradually covering the ruins in a thick layer of soil. As if this were not enough, in the Middle Ages the Alpheios changed its course and ran for a while right through the middle of the Altis, thus adding silt to complete the process by which the site was hidden. However, it was exactly this process which helped to preserve the antiquities until 1829, when investigation of the site began.

The site today lies in a peaceful fertile valley. We begin our tour of the area from the south west entrance to the Altis, near the Museum. We pass the Prytaneion, a building contemporary with the temple of Zeus, where, on the fifth and final day of the Games, the victors of the various events took part in a banquet. The Heraion, dedicated to Hera, is the oldest Greek temple yet found — it dates from the middle of the 7th century B.C. The circular Philippeion had five chryselephantine statues: of the Macedonian King Philip, his parents Amyntas and Eurydice, his wife Olympias and his son Alexander. The Pelopeion was sacred to Pelops, and the Metroon to Rhea-Cybele.

The temple of Hera, in the secos of which the Hermes of Praxiteles was found.

The Philippeio, a religious building constructed by the family of Alexander the Great.

The Paionios Victory (reconstruction).

The Exedra of Herod Atticus was a semi-circular aqueduct which was decorated with much statuary. The treasuries were small buildings in the shape of temples where costly votive offerings were deposited. We can still see the bases of the bronze statues of Zeus erected out of fines imposed on athletes who cheated. The Stadium had room for 45,000 spectators, and the running-track is 192 metres long, as compared to the classical 186 m. Just outside is the Echo Colonnade, built in the 4th century, where it is said that each sound was repeated seven times. The famous temple of Zeus was built in the 5th century by the Elian architect Libon, and in its sekos stood the gigantic statue of Zeus, the work of Phidias. The Bouleuterion was the seat of the Olympic Parliament. The Leonidaion was the ancient site's official hotel. There is a Byzantine church on the site of Phidias' workshop. The Theokoleon was the residence of the priests, and there are also remains of the Palaestra, the Gymnasium and various Roman buildings.

The Archaeological Museum contains the famous Praxiteles Hermes, the Victory of Paeonius, Mycenean ceramic artefacts, a rich collection of copper votive offerings from the Geometric and Archaic periods, works of Archaic sculpture from the pediments and metopes of the temple of Zeus, parts of the structure of the temples of Zeus and Hera, ceramic figurines from the pre-Classical period, Roman sculpture, etc. There is also a philatelic museum, with stamps which have the Olympics as their theme, photographs of famous personalities, albums and other printed material concerning the modern Olympics, and much more.

The Hermes of Praxiteles.

The entrance to the Stadium and, below the ancient Stadium of Olympia itself.

The Early Christian basilica on the site of Pheidias workshop.

The road continues east from Olympia.

We pass through **Miraka;** archaeologists place ancient **Pisa** between here and the Alpheios.

Indeed, remains of a prehistoric acropolis have been found on a small hill nearby. According to tradition, Pisa was the centre of a federal state which included the cities of Salmone, Herakleia, Arpinne, Kykesio and Dyspontio. The state was founded by Oenomaus, who was later displaced by Pelops (for details, see above, p. 11) and originally had the privilege of organising the Olympic Games.

After many years of struggle between Pisa and the Elians (notably in 588-572) the Elians took the city and destroyed it, thus winning the privilege for themselves. The former inhabitants of the town allied themselves with the Arcadians, however, and in 364 managed to win back their rights. Indeed, they confiscated the treasures of the temple of Zeus and minted gold and copper coins to pay their armies. Unfortunately for them, though, the Elians went on the offensive again, defeated the Pisans, and declared the 104th Olympiad, which the Pisans had organised, null and void. After that, Pisa drops out of history.

Goings eastwards, the road leads to **Louvro,** and then **Vasilaki** (altitude 350 metres), where a minor road branches off to the north through Xirokambos, Nemouta, Lala, and so on.

The main road continues further to the east and at the Koklamas bridge enters the Prefecture of Arcadia, leading to Vytina-Tripoli (see page 114).

33. Pyrgos - Andritsaina
(63 kms)

The main road to Andritsaina leaves Pyrgos to the south east. After 3 kilometres we cross the Alpheios on a bridge which is the boundary of the province of Olympia.

After 5 kilometres we come to **Agoulinitsa (Epitalio)** near which there is a monastery (Zoodochos Pighi) among pines and streams. On a hill to the north of the village stood the prehistoric town of **Thryon** or **Thryoussa** or **Alpheian Poros**, which is mentioned by Homer. In the historical period, it was called Epitalion.

To the right (east) of the road lies the shallow lagoon of Epitalios, which produces eels. We reach **Anemochori**. There is a fine view over the lake, and a pine wood at Strofylia, where there are fine beaches.

Remains of the ancient city of **Arene** (otherwise known as Makistou) have been found at the nearby village of **Samiko**. Most of the city lies under the lagoon, but well-preserved sections of the walls can be seen. The view from the ancient acropolis over the plain and the Ionian is pleasant. The most important find from the site are in the Olympia Museum.

At the village of Samiko, 28 kilometres from Pyrgos, a detour from the main road to the east leads to the town of **Krestena**.

A minor road leads north, through the large village of **Makrysia**. A Mycenean graveyard has been found at **Kania**, nearby, and find from the tholos tombs can be seen in the Museum at Olympia.

The ancient city of **Skillous** lay between Krestena, Makrysia and the village of Ladiko. A large part of the city's land was given to the exiled Athenian writer Xenophon, who wrote many of his most important works there. The writer had a temple to Ephesian Artemis built near the river Selinous, and financed the project with the spoils he had gained from his campaign in Asia. The temple was in the same shape as the Artemisium at Ephesus, and was built of Pentelic marble.

Ruins of the ancient city and of a temple which may be this same one have been found near the village of **Skyllountia** (Mazi), and sculpures from the temple are in the Archaeological Museum at Patra. There are also remains of an Early Christian basilica in the same area.

The main road to Andritsaina, from Krestena to the east, continues, climbing up the slopes of Mt Minthis. We pass through **Grylos** and **Greka**, and then enter **Platiana**. Half an hour to the west of Platiana (through pleasant scenery, well-wooded and with a fine view) are the ruins of the prehistoric city of **Aipy**, which is mentioned by Homer.

The city is walled and fortified in the Mycenean way, and there are remains of the palace, the agora, a theatre, temples, and a fort. The city was important during the years of the Achaean League.

At about 65 kms from Pyrgos to the south west, we come to the at-

Agoulinitsa among its pines and olive trees.

tractive town of **Andritsaina**, on the slopes of Mt Minthis. The town is watered by a mountain stream, and has many fine fountains, often with multiple spouts. The finest, with four spouts, was erected in 1724. The fine scenery and the cool climate attract many visitors.

History would seem to indicate that there was a town here before the Frankish period. During Turkish rule the inhabitants were largely Christian, and the town school was famed throughout the area. It was open continuously from 1796. The churches are of special interest: St Therapon (15th century), St Athanasius (18th century), St Barbara (18th century), and St Nicholas (18th century). Nearby is the monastery of Our Lady 'Sepetio-tissa' (12th century) and the castle of Zakoukas, which stands at a height of 1,340 m. The town's library contains a most important collection of early editions (16th century Venetian and Vatican), as well as many fascinating documents relating to the history of the Greek Revolution. The library was founded in 1840, by a gift from K. Nikolopoulos, and contains some 20,000 volumes.

A road south 'from Andritsaina leads through wild scenery to the temple at **Bassae**. The temple is to Apollo Epikourios, and is a Doric peripteron. It was restored at the beginning of the century.

Built by Ictinus in about 421 B.C., the temple was planned, according to Pausanias, to honour Apollo, who as

Andritsaina, famous for its fountains.

The temple of Epicurean Apollo at Bassae, Figalia.

'epikourios' (helper) assisted the Phigaleians to save themselves from an epidemic during the Peloponnesian War. However, finds from the area have shown that the god honoured here was originally a warrior, and it may be that Bassae was used as a gathering point and advanced position by the locals in their conflicts with the Spartans. Systematic restoration of the temple began in 1987.

There would appear to have been an earlier temple on nearly the same site, and at the nearby site of **Koumbia** (where there is a marvellous view) other temples, perhaps to Aphrodite and Artemis, have been discovered.

The main road leads on to the east from Andritsaina to Karytaina and Megalopolis (see p. 105).

Other, minor, roads lead to the villages of **Plateia, Perivolia** and **Figalia** (Pavlitsa). Near the last village walls and remains of buildings from the ancient city of **Phigaleia** have been found, near the boundaries of Arcadia, Elia and Messinia. Its acropolis was where the village of **Ayios Ilias** now stands. Coins and pottery have been found here. On the slope forming the bank of the river Nedas remains of links and the scars left by thick rope can be made out. They are a reminder that in ancient times the river was navigable as far as the ancient acropolis of Phigaleia, where the boats tied up.

The road passes through the villages of **Kalitsaina, Platania, Avlona** and **Sidirokastro** and meets up with the main Pyrgos-Kyparissia road. The river Nedas is the boundary between Elia and Messinia.

34. Loutra Kaïafa - Messinia (19 kms)

Twenty eight kilometress south east of Pyrgos, at Samiko, the main road continues south, passing along the shores of lakes Agoulinitsa, Epitalios and Kaïafa.

The buildings of **Loutra Kaïafa** stand on a small island (St Catherine) in the lake of the same name, which is linked to the mainland by a bridge. The medicinal properties of the waters were known in ancient times, when neither beach nor lake existed and the sea reached into the caves of Mt Smerna (Lapithos) from which the waters spring.

Kaiafa Lake with its medicinal springs and t Zacharo, founded in 1860, a

There is a myth that the Centaurs sought refuge here to heal their wounds from the arrows of Heracles, which had been dipped in the poison of the Lernaean Hydra. This explains the somewhat off-putting stench of the water.

More recent traditions link the name with the judge of Christ, Caiaphas, who, shipwrecked and injured, tried to reach the springs to heal himself. The waters, however, refused to have anything to do with him, and their smell drove him away.

There are two springs, and their waters are efficacious in the treatment of skin diseases, conditions of the liver and gall bladder, arthritis and gynaecological complaints.

The surrounding area is lushly vegetated and offers good hunting. Eel may be fished in the lake (after one has provided oneself with the necessary permit).

rofylia pine wood.
agricultural area, the ancient Plain of Pylos.

The main road continues south, along the coast, and soon enters **Zacharo**, an important commercial and agricultural centre.

We continue south, and a minor road soon leads to the right to **Kakovatos**, where the German archaeologist Dörpfeld investigated Mycenean tholos tombs, buildings and a splendid palace. He claimed this as the site of prehistoric Triphyllian Pylos, which is mentioned in the Homeric epics. Some of the finds from the site may be seen in the Athens Archaeological Museum.

Four kilometres from the Kakovatos turning, the main road passes through **Tholo.**

A minor road from here takes us east to **Kato Figalia** (Zourtsa) and **Lepreo**. There was an ancient city of the same name on this site, taking its name from the mythical hero Leprius, son of Pyrgeus. The city was first inhabited by Caucones, who were of Pelasgian stock, then by Thessalians, followed by Minyans and Elians. Today we can see ruins of the walls, a temple, the acropolis (at Paliopyrgos) and various other buildings. The Kefalovryso spring may be the famous ancient spring of Arene.

The main road continues south along the coast from Tholo and soon enters **Yannitsochori**, which is the last village in Elia before Messinia.

MESSINIA

Messinia lies in the south-western corner of the Peloponnese. Its capital, Kalamata, is famous for its olives, and for its circular dance (known as the 'kalamatianos') danced by pretty girls whose hands are linked by the silk kerchiefs for which the town is also known. Messinia, with the sea on three sides, land of wise king Nestor of Pylos, whom Homer describes, land of Navarino, where a historic seabattle placed the seal on the Greek victory over the Turks, is as light and airy a place as the music for the 'kalamatianos'.

The natural surroundings of Messinia are warm and mild. There are verdant areas, long sandy beaches and others with round pebbles, pine-woods close to the coast, sheltered bays and, up on Taigetos, cool mountain villages. The gods have been kind to this part of the Peloponnese, scattering beauties generously across its 2,990 square kilometres.

The area has been inhabited since prehistoric times. It was on Messinian soil that the second large state in the Peloponnese developed. Its king was Nestor, a figure of venerable age by the time of the Homeric poems. His wooden palace must have been burned down by a sudden fire, and it lay for thousands of years beneath the ashes before the archaeologists cast light on its ruins once more. With it, they found 2,500 codices and 1,200 tablets incribed in Linear B script.

In historical times, fertile Messinia was one of Sparta's principal aspirations. There were three wars between Messinia and Sparta, and in the end the Messinians were forced to emigrate. They built a new city in Italy, on the site of the former city of Zangle, and called it Messinia.

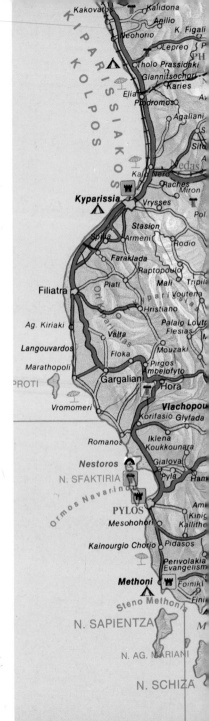

Map of the Prefecture of Messinia

Those who were left behind became helots: slaves of the Spartans. Later, in 371 BC, the Athenians and the Macedonians helped the Messinans to recapture the coastline between Taigetus and Cape Tainaron. The Messinians allied themselves to Rome, which annexed them in 146 BC. The Frankish castle of Kalamata is testimony to the fact that Western invaders passed this way. The castle, built by Geoffey de Villehardouin, was the birthplace of Princess Isabella or Isambo, whose troubled life came down to later generations as a kind of fairy-tale before Angelos Terzakis re-worked it in a novel and made it part of modern Greek literature. But the Franks were not the only invaders of Messinia: the Venetians left their mark here, too. The large Venetian castles of Methoni and Koroni are witnesses to the power which Venice once had in this area. That of Methoni is one of the largest and the finest castles in Greece. The two castles face out to sea at either corner of the western-most promontory of the Peloponnese. The sea over which they look seems to have been a more familiar element to the Messinians, and to have been more important for them, than is the case elsewhere along the coast of the Peloponnese. In Koroni, for example, one could almost imagine oneself in a Cycladic town. The white-painted cobbled streets wind uphill between little houses painted white, yellow and purple, with the windows picked out in blue or red. Pylos, too, is reminisscent of an island township.

Although many of the inhabitants of Messinia are engaged in occupations related to the sea, the majority still work the land. The olive tree and its fruit and oil provide work for many families, but general farming is highly developed, with production of lemons, oranges, cotton, rice, figs, potatoes, wine, and vegetables. This is one of the reasons why Messinia has retained its population; with more than 159,000 inhabitants, the Perfecture is, with Ileia, the second most densely inhabited in the Peloponnese, after Achaia. Around Kalamata there is also a considerable amount of industrial development, particularly in the processing of olives, olive oil, alcohol, soap, etc., which has also contributed to maintaining the population at a constant level.

The local costume of the Kalamata area (Alagonia).

Kyparissia, mentioned in the Homeric epics, and its medieval castle.

35. Kyparissia

The main road from Elia continues along the coast and enters Messinia. At about 14 kms there is a fork at the village of **Kalo Nero**. The branch to the east leads to the villages of Kato Kopanaki, Kalliroi and Allagi and then joins the main Tripoli-Megalopoli-Kalamata road (see p. 99 and 160).

The part of the road which continues south soon enters **Kyparissia**, an important urban centre which stands on the site of ancient **Kyparisseis**, which is mentioned by Homer. Strabo and other writers refer to the town by its modern name or slight variations of it. In the early days, it was a Spartan colony, but the Messenians annexed it in the fourth century. It became a member of the Achaean League in 191. In the Mid-dle Ages, the town was called Arkadia, perhaps from the large numbers of Arcadians who sought refuge there from Slav invaders. Under the Franks, it was a separate barony of the Villehardouins, along with Kalamata, although later it split off from the other town and formed at barony of its own, belonging to the d'Onois family. The locals played an important part in the War of Independence, and their town was almost completely destroyed by Ibrahim when he occupied it in 1825.

The town today consists of two parts — the Upper Town (Ano Poli), built on the lower Slopes of Mt Psichro, and the sea-front (Paralia), built along the shores of the Gulf of Kyparissia. There are also ruins of a medieval castle on a hill overlooking the town.

36. Kyparissia - Pylos
(62 kms)

East of Kyparissia, at **Peristera** near the village of **Mira**, an important early Mycenean tomb has been excavated. The objects found in it show the relations between the Myceneans and Minoan Crete.

Nine kilometres south west of Kyparissia the main road reaches **Agrili**, where there is a church of the Dormition of the Virgin reputedly built by Thomas Palaeologue, Despot of the Peloponnese.

Filiatra lies about 72 kilometres from Pyrgos. The town stands in a plain notable for vineyards, olive groves, market gardens and orchards, and there is good hunting to be had in the mountains round about and plenty of fish in the sea. From the Dexameni hill there is a good view.

In the town, the sights are the town clock, which is in a high tower, and a model of the Eiffel Tower, built with the money of a local resident who emigrated to the United States.

The town was built in the 16th century and has old churches, such as the pretty 18th century chapel of St George, with wall paintings, and the church of Our Lady 'Gouviotissa'.

The Museum, housed in a room next to the Town Hall, contains icons and Early Christian sculpture from churches in the area.

There are local celebrations for the feast day of St Charalambos (10 February), who is the patron saint of the town. On St George's Day there are the Lelonian Horse Races, in memory of Panagos Lelonis, a local

horseman who was killed by his Turkish opponents in the years before the Revolution. On hearing the news of his death, his fiancée mounted his horse and rode it into the sea, thus ending the life of both of them. Another Filiatra woman committed suicide to escape the Turks. In about 1700 Helen Skordakopoula jumped off a rock with her child in her arms rather than submit to their attentions. A marble cross stands on the spot where she ended her life.

A road south east from Filiatra leads to **Christiani**, at 640 metres. This is the medieval Christianoupolis, which was the seat of a bishop from the 12th century until the War of Independence. Amvrosios Fanzis, historian of the Revolution, was attached to the bishopric here. The magnificent church of Ayia Sotira, of the 11th century, destroyed by earthquake in 1886 and regarded as one of the finest Byzantine churches in Greece, has been restored.

In a cave 2.5 kilometres from Filiatra to the south east stands the old church of St Christopher, with inscriptions. The coast road to Ayia kyriaki continues to the south and reaches **Marathos** or Marathoupoli, the port for Gargaliani.

The main road leaves Filiatra to the south west and passes though the Eforokampos plain in the direction of a modern agricultural centre whose development began in the last century — **Gargaliani**.

There is a library built with bequest from Dr Sortiris Briskas, who made his name in France.

Opposite Maratho is the pretty little island of **Proti**, which, in former times, was a haunt of corsairs, among them the dreaded Patoulias.

There are many tales of buried treasure on the island, and much fruitless sweat has been shed in attempts to find it.

On the western side of the island the bollards of the pirate ships can be seen. To the norht of Proti, on the rocks above Grammenos Bay, are numerous inscriptions carved by the sailors of ancient and modern times, giving the names of their ships.

The main road leads east from Gargaliani. Nearby, at an altitude of 240 metres, is the village of **Floka** or **Pyrgos**. The approach through attractive hilly country. This area has been inhabited since very early times. Archaeological investigations have revealed important finds from the Pro-Mycenean and Mycenean periods.

Peristeria: a Mycenean tholos tomb.

The road continues round bends and enters the village of **Chora**, which has an archaeological museum which houses the finds from the Palace of Nestor.

The spot known as Kefalovryso is especially worth visiting — it has aged plane trees which cast deep shadow, an unusual church and an aqueduct which collects its plentiful water.

Chora has become well-known in the last twenty years as the approach to Nestor's Palace, which stands on the hill known as Epano Eglianou, to the South West of the town. Every summer, artistic events are held in Chora, under the general name of 'Nestoria'.

The palace area is the largest of its kind in mainland Greece. There were four basic buildings, and a large number of auxiliary structures. The central building has a monumental propylon (gate), a courtyard, a throne-room and corridors leading to nearby storehouses. The building was two-storeyed, and the royal family lived on the upper floor.

Among the most significant finds are those from a small room next to the central gate, which was used as a records office. The finds consist of a large number of clay tablets inscribed in Linear B, charred by the destructive fire which ruined the palace in about 1200 BC. They seem to concern accounts, and their texts prove the existence of Greek inhabitants in the area with a Greek script.

The second building is older, according to archaeologists, and was used

The archaeological site of the Palace of Nestor.

as a residence for the crown prince or the king's mother.

A large piece of pumice with plaster decorations, found in a seven-roomed building to the south east of the acropolis, seems to have been an altar, and the building may well have been the palace workshops.

A large storeroom with oil jars has been discovered on the south west edge of the hill. At many points, the walls stand to a height of one metre, and the central rooms must have been richly decorated in plaster and paint.

Significant finds have also been made in the people's quarter around the hill. A large tholos tomb stands to the north east of the hill. Examples of pottery, wall-paintings, household utensils, gold jewellery, Linear B tablets and other objects from the site may be seen in the extremely interesting Museum at Chora and in the Archaeological Museum in Athens.

The main road from Chora turns south, passes the archaeological site and continues towards the Gulf of Pylos. From **Koryfasio** a minor road leads to the seaside village of **Romanou**.

Eglianos: Mycenean tholos tomb.

The hearth in the Palace of Nestor.

The bath, in the bathroom.

Further to the south the main road draws nearer the coast. We pass through **Yialova** and there is a branch to the left, which leads to Messini and Kalamata.

The West turn goes on to Pylos, a picturesque town built in a semi-circle round its harbour and formerly known as Navarino.

The bay on which **Pylos** is built is protected from wind and weather by the island of Sfaktiria. This is a modern settlement, and has no connection with the ancient city of Neleus and Nestor, the site of which was near Chora (see above).

When Mycenean Pylos was destroyed, the inhabitants re-settled on Cape Koryfasio, opposite Pylos. But after the Second Messenian War the Pylians abandoned their city and moved to Cyllene. The site remained empty until 425, when the Athenians built a small fort and posted a garrison under Demosthenes. This fell into Spartan hands towards the end of the Peloponnesian War.

Later, the Messenians moved in, and Pausanias says that in his time (2nd Century AD) the city had a temple to Coryphasian Athena and the tomb of Nestor, while nearby, at Voidokilia, was a cave which was believed to have been the stable for Nestor's oxen.

In 1296, the city, by now known as Navarino, belonged to Nicholas II St Omer, who built the castle, in which Gascons and Navarins ensconsed themselves in the century which followed.

The famous sea-battle of Navarino took place on 20 October 1827, and saw the Turkish and Egyptian fleets utterly defeated by the combined forces of Britain, France and Russia. Pylos was eventually taken by the French in September 1828 and handed over to the Greeks, though the French, under the engineer Maison, stayed on to help plan the new town. The castle may be seen on the hill above the town and there is an interesting church of the Transfiguration inside the walls.

The lovely Pylos.

The Bay of Voidokoilia.

The Museum of Pylos has a collection containing pottery, a ceramic basin, gold pots, jewellery and other objects of the Mycenean period (from digs at Peristeria), pottery and glass artefacts from the Hellenistic period, Roman bronze statues, and a fine collection of engravings which belonged to the Frenchman Reynier Piot.

In the middle of the fine natural harbour of Pylos is the rocky island of Marathonissi, or Chelonaki, on which there is a memorial to the English dead of the sea-battle.

Sfaktiria, the long narrow island which all but closes the gulf, has impressive caves and grottoes (to the south west).

The gun emplacements of Ibrahim and Tsamados may still be seen, and there are monuments to the dead of April 1825, Santaroza, one of the Philhellenes, and the Russian sailors killed in the battle, together with a memorial to Paule-Marie Bonaparte, nephew of Napoleon.

The neighbouring rock of **Tsichli-Baba** has a lighthouse, a monument to the French dead and a large natural rock arch with 144 steps (which used to be a pirate hide-out).

On the mainland (at Pilos), to the north of Sfaktiria are ruins of walls and Demosthenes' well, mosaics and, to the north, the castle of Navarino built by Nicholas II St Omer.

Nestor's Cave may be seen nearby. Mycenean graves have been found at the little harbour of Voidokilia.

A minor road leads from Pylos to the east, to the village of **Kinigos**.

The Bourtzi at Methoni.

37. Pylos - Methoni - Koroni (49 kms)

The Methoni road climbs out of Pylos to the south, following the coast. About one kilometre before we reach the town is a 1st or 2nd century catacomb and a small Byzantine church (St Basil).

Methoni is perhaps best known for its impressive castle, which the visitor should on no account miss. The Homeric name was Pedasos and the poet states that it was one of the seven towns given to Achilles by Agamemnon to appease his anger after the bearing off of Briseïs.

The name 'Methoni' derives from a beautiful but mythical daughter of

Oeneus, and the area seems to have been given by the Spartans to settlers from Nafplio in very early times.

Athens besieged it unsuccessfully in 431. The town flourished most, however, in the Middle Ages, when its geographical position and its fine natural harbour helped it to become an important staging-post on trade routes between Europe and the East. The Byzantines used the town as a stronghold against pirates, and in 1204 Methoni was the starting-point for the Franks on their conquest of the whole Peloponnese.

The town was surrendered to the Venetians in 1209, by the Treaty of Sapienza, and they stayed for nearly three centuries, turning the town into an important commercial, naval and cultural centre. The Venetians built the fine castle on the foundations of the ancient acropolis. The octagonal tower, known as Bourtzi, which stands to the south of the castle and is linted to the mainland by a bridge, is a later Turkish addition to the defences.

In August 1500, 100,000 Turks under Sultan Bayezid laid siege to the town. After it fell into his hands, he ordered all the men to be slaughtered and the women and children sent into slavery.

The Knights of Malta held Methoni for a while in the mid-16th century, and the Venetians returned again from 1686 to 1715. Later it passed into the hands of the Turks, with whom it remained until the liberation of Greece. In 1825 it was the base for Ibrahim Pasha when, in

The shallow sandy bay of Methoni, and the medieval castle.

revenge against the freedom-fighters, he devastated the Peloponnese. In 1828, Methoni was eventually liberated by French troops.

The castle is in excellent condition. Its state of completeness makes it one of the best-preserved medieval buildings in Europe. On the outside various coats of arms can be seen, including those of the Genoese and the Venetians' lion of St Mark. Next to the harbour there is a fine clean beach. Fish abound. At the beginning of Lent the locals hold a festival with a village mask wedding as its centrepiece.

Off Methoni to the south lie the **Oinoussai Islands**: Sapienza, which has a large lighthouse, Ayia Mariani and Schiza, which has an impressive cave with stalactites and stalagmites.

A minor road leading east from Methoni takes us through **Phinikounta** (the name is from the ancient harbour), **Akritochori, Yameia** and **Falanthi** before bringing us out on the Koroni-Kalamata road near **Harokopio**.

Koroni is built on the site of ancient **Asine**. The ancient town of Korone was established in 365 BC by Epimelides, who came from Coronea in Boeotia, on the site of the even older city of **Aepeia** or **Pedasos**, which is mentioned in Homer. This position was somewhat to the south west of the modern town, on the road leading to Vasilitsi (the most southerly village on Cape Akritas).

The town became independent and produced its own coinage, joining the Achaean League in 184 BC. The next year the Messenians tried to re-take it, but without success. Thus it remained in the League until the 3rd century AD.

It was removed to its present position in the Middle Ages, and became an important commercial centre. It was taken by the Franks in 1205, but the Venetians captured it the following year and used it as a supply base for their fleet.

Documents of the period refer to Koroni as a fine and strong city, with significant exports of high-quality olive oil, from its fertile hinterland. There was also a certain amount of industry, producing metalwork, dyes and siege machinery which was among the most sought-after in Europe between the 14th and 16th centuries.

There was a ship supply centre, and business seems to have been so profitable that in the 13th century Koroni and Methoni together sent 2,000 ounces of gold to Venice every year, from their excess profits.

The Turks under Sultan Bayezid, took the town in 1500, and held it until the War of Independence, although the Venetians managed to recapture it for short periods on two occasions.

1828 Koroni, too, was taken from the Turks by the French who had fought at Navarino, and landed it over to the Greeks.

Of its former greatness, however, all that remains is the popular saying that you will succeed in business only "if you have an uncle in Koroni".

The impressive castle contains ruins of the Byzantine church 'Of the Divine Wisdom', which was the seat of the local bishops.

There is also a nunnery (of St John) within the castle boundaries and a church of St Haralambos.

Under the walls to the south is the wood of Our Lady 'Eleistra', with a church containing unusual icons of St Luke, the Crucifixion and Our Lady.

The nearby beach at **Zanga** attracts many Greek and foreign tourists, and the sea is rich in fish.

The small museum at Koroni contains finds from the surrounding area (vessels, column capitals, coins, Byzantine vestments, etc.).

he view of now sleepy Koroni once a mighty medieval town.

38. Koroni - Ancient Messene (58 kms)

The road from Koroni to the north passes through a small fertile plain.

Ten kilometres before Kalamata is **Messini**, from which there is an air service to Athens.

The town is often referred to as **Nisi** (island), a name which has survived from the time when the river Pamisos ran round the town or in a moat around the Frankish castle whose ruins can still be seen. The castle was one of the Villehardouin family's residences. The town was liberated from the Turks in 1828.

It has organised beaches, with sand, at **Bouka** (which has camp sites) and **Velika**. There are festivities here on the first Monday of Lent (carnival), St John's day (with dancing, singing and roast food around the fires which always accompany this particular feast day) and at Easter (with paper aeroplane contests and prizes for the winers). The surrounding countryside is good for hunting.

Messini today has no connection with the ancient city of the same name. The ancient settlement which stood on the site of Messini was called Makaria.

Five kilometress north of Messini a road which leaves **Triodos** to the west leads to the villages of **Vromovrysi, Agrilia** and **Androusa**.

In the Middle Ages, Androusa was one of the most important towns in Messinia, with a fortified castle and well-developed trade.

In 1308 it was the see of a bishop and under the Turks it was the capital of a province. Its last bishop, Joseph, became modern Greece's first Minister of Education and his statue stands in the village square.

Here there is a single-nave Byzantine church of St George (restored) and the ruins of the castle and aqueduct.

Nearby, before the village of **Ellinoklisia**, is the Samarina Monastery (the name is a corruption of the Frankish 'Santa Maria'). According to tradition it was built by the Empress Theodora, when she was in exile, on the ruins of an ancient temple. It is dedicated to Our Lady as the Life-Giving Spring ('Zoodochos Pighi').

Near the village of **Mankaniako** is the 'Adriomonastiro' (monastery), built by Andronicus Palaeologue and dedicated to the Transfiguration. A spring below the sanctuary of its church supplies Androusa with water.

The road continues north from Messini and passes through the villages of **Eva, Hania** and **Lambaina**. According to ancient tradition, Dionysus and his followers held their orgiastic celebrations on the mountain above Eva and the name is supposed to be derived from their shouts of 'evoi-evan'.

Before the village of Lambaina the main road forks and the north western branch leads to the village of **Mavromati**, at a height of 395 metres. This is an attractive and green village built in amphitheatre style on the southern slopes of Mt Ithomi (Vulcanos).

Near Mavromati are the ruins of

The Odeum of ancient Messene, with the village of Mavromati in the background.

Ancient Messene (Ithome), the most important ancient city in the area. Its acropolis was on the peak of Mt Ithomi and it was strongly fortified, which enabled it to hold the Spartans at bay for many years before finally having to give in.

In 464 BC the inhabitants rebelled and walled themselves up in the ancient city, which held out for a further ten years and which the Spartans required the help of Athens to recapture. Among the famous figures produced by Messene were Aristomenes (who refused the title of king), and King Aristodemus.

The later Messene was founded in 369 by Epaminondas at Mavromati, and the new town joined the Achaean League in 180.

Excavations have unearthed a fine theatre, a stadium, the Agora and other buildings, as well as many fascinating daily objects and works of art.

Pausanias says that there were 30 temples in the town. The Church of St Nicholas (at the cemetery) stands on the site of a temple of Poseidon. The spring under the plane trees in the village is believed to be the ancient Clepsydra, and nearby can be seen the remains of the Arcadian Gates built by Epaminondas.

The musem in Mavromati has interesting sculpture, architectural fragments and important Hellenistic and Roman inscriptions.

East of Mavromati, at a short distance is the Vulcanos Monastery, at a height of 520 metres, the original buildings of which stood on Mt Ithomi, on the site of an altar to Zeus where human sacrifice is said to have been practised. The Zeus altar was a sanctuary for slaves, and the priest had the right to declare free all those who sought refuge there.

A more modern tradition tells of some hermits from Mt Eva, facing the site, who, during a terrible storm one night, saw an icon of the Virgin hanging on a tree and lit by a lantern.

In about 375 they built a monastery on the site, called Katholiko, or 'Our Lady of the Peak', which was rebuilt in the 17th century with murals by the Moschos brothers.

There are also three interesting chapels: that of St John has fine murals of the 17th and 18th centuries, some of which are among the most outstanding examples of Byzantine art, while a small but priceless icon which is now housed in the new 'Kato' monastery is reputed to be by St Luke. The icon is silver-coated and beautifully carved.

Near the main church there is a chasm which emits hot air in the winter and cold in the summer.

From the fork near the village of **Lambaina** the road east continues to the town of **Meligalas**, built in the Byzantine period. Its chief landmark is a tall stone clock tower on the Profitis Ilias hill. This hill was in ancient times the look-out post for the inhabitants of the ancient city of **Steny-claros** (its ruins are nearby, to the north west).

The geographical position of Meligalas (originally built around the 12th century Church of the Archangels) has favoured its development as a commercial, agricultural and craft industry centre which has made the most of the plain's natural wealth in agricultural produce, particularly in vines, olives and fig trees.

A little to the west of Meligalas, at the confluence of three rivers, is the picturesque triple bridge of Mavrozoumena, haunted, it is said, like the bridge of Arta, by the ghost of a young girl who was buried alive in its foundations to ensure its stability. It rests on the remains of an ancient bridge.

North of Meligalas, after **Zevgolatio**, the road enters the village of **Ichalia**, built near the site of an ancient settlement of the same name. According to tradition, **Ancient Oichalia** was founded by Melaneus, son of Apollo, who gave it the name of his wife. Rites similar to the Eleusinian mysteries took place in the sacred wood of Demeter and Persephone, which was on the site now occupied by the village of **Filia**.

The road joins the main Tripoli-Megalopoli-Kalamata road at the village of **Allaghi**.

The castle of Kalamata from the north.

Kalamata

Kalamata as a city dates from the Middle Ages, although it was built near the site of the ancient city of **Pherae** or **Pharae**, which is mentioned in Homer.

It took its name from the monastery of Our Lady of Kalamata (the alternative, formal, name of Kalamai belonged to an ancient village which Pausanias mentions as having stood in the area, but certainly not on the site of the present city).

History begins for Kalamata in the early 13th century, when William de Champlitte divided the Peloponnese into twelve baronies and offered that of Kalamata to his associate Geoffrey de Villehardouin.

The Villehardouin family built a castle there and had their family tomb installed, despite the fact that as princes of Achaea they were supposed to have their seat in Andravida. When the last of the family died in 1278 and the barony began to decline, the strong castle was bitterly fought over by Franks, Slavs and Byzantines, until it was finally acquired by Constantine Palaeologue at the beginning of the 15th century. He, however, did not enjoy it long, for the city was forced to pay tribute to the Turks in 1446 and was taken by them in 1460.

Under the relative peace of Turkish occupation, the town grew rich on the products of the fertile plain and thanks to the industrial flair of the locals.

177

Kalamata: the cathedral.

A loom in the castle nunnery.

After a brief spell under the Venetians, Kalamata took part enthusiastically in the Orloff revolt (1769) and was severely punished for its presumption by the Turks.

The town was among the first to be freed during the 1821 Revolution, and a Messinian Senate was formed on 23 March of that year. The first newspaper to be published on Greek soil was issued in Kalamata in August, 1821.

The events of 1821 are celebrated on 23 March each year, and in May there is a flower festival with exhibition in the castle, proces ions of floats, theatrical performances, etc.

Inside the imposing castle can be seen the remains of Mycenean, Roman, Hellenistic, Frankish, Venetian, Byzantine and Turkish buildings.

The small Byzantine church of Our Lady of Kalamata stands at the top near the tourist pavilion, with a fine view over the Gulf of Messinia, the plain and Mt Taïyetos. In the city is the church of the Apostles, built by Andronicus Palaeologue in 1317. There are paintings inside the dome, which forms part of the modern church, and a ruinous Frankish belltower. This is the church in which the

An alley in the Municipal Market.

Messinian Senate was formed. The Cathedral built in 1859, has another icon reputedly by St Luke.

The nunnery (18th century), under the castle is the centre of the silk-weaving industry, and ancient and modern looms may be seen. There is a Byzantine church in the neighbouring cemetery. The beach is a good one.

A neo-Classical house by Ziller, on the seafront.

Kalamata and its seafront, seen from Taigetos.

The helmet of a fighter in the War of Independence.

The archaeological museum of Kalamata, which is housed in the Benaki mansion, contains a collection of stone tools and Neolithic pottery from sites at Malthi, Mycenean, proto-Geometric and Geometric pottery, Mycenean figurines from Karpofora, Achaean and Hellenistic pottery, late Classical, Hellenistic and Roman statuary, a floor mosaic from Roman times, late-Byzantine icons, folk embroidery and relics of famous local families from the years of the Revolution.

There is also a Cathedral Museum, with icons, church vessels, Gospels and vestments, and a Historical and Folk Museum, with weapons, household utensils, examples of folk art and paintings on the subject of the War of Independence.

The town's intellectual life is headed by the People's Library (40,000 volumes) and the Association for the Propagation of Learning, which runs the Historical and Folk Museum.

39. Kalamata - Kardamyli
(37 kms)

A road emerges from Kalamata in a southeasterly direction and soon enters the famous Mani region, beginning at the outer or Messinian Mani (see p. 205).

Four kilometres away, at Yannitsanika, the climb of Mt Selitsa starts, leading to the beauty of the site of the Timiova Monastery, among plane trees, walnut trees and rushing streams. The monastery (which has a guesthouse) was built in the 8th century and possesses a miraculous icon of the Virgin. It was burnt down in the Orloff uprising and bombarded by the Germans during the Second World War.

Just before **Selitsa** and **Almiros**, in a gorge about 7 kilometres from Kalamata, the remains of a wall can be seen near the sea. This is the Wall of Verga, about 1,500 metres long, built by the Greeks in 1826 to impede Ibrahim's troops on their march into the Mani.

There is a fine beach at Almiros, with the houses of Selitsa climbing up a nearby hillside. The first Maniot tower, at Palaiochora, can be seen in the distance.

A beehive tomb and the ruins of a temple have been found at **Kambos**, to the south (420 metres), above which are the remains of the castle of Zarnata, which was the medieval name for the whole area, on the peak of a steep rock. The later tower of Koumoundouraki (or Koumoundourou) crowns another rock. The

Church of Zoodochos Pighi nearby has interesting wall paintings and a wooden screen. The view over the Gulf of Messinia, the plain and Mt. Taïyetos is superb.

Further to the south at 37 kms., on the coast, we come to **Kardamyli**, another Homeric name. There was an acropolis in this typically Maniot village, and many temples. Under the control of Macedon, the city became independent and after 146 belonged to the Community of Free Laconians. The Emperor Augustus gave it to Sparta as a port. The village today has ruins of the acropolis, the tombs of the Heavenly Twins (two parallel shafts in the rock) a church of St Spyridon (6th century) with wall paintings, some remains of the 12th century castle and five Maniot towers. Ten kms to the

The church of St Spyridon (12th century).

Historic Kardamili, with its pebbly beach in the background.

northeast of Kardamyle is the gorge of **Viros,** one of the largest and most impressive in Greece.

Continuing south, we reach **Ayios Nikolaos**, with a good beach and fine hunting and fishing. There are some Maniot towers and a church of St Nicholas. The cave of 'Katafigi' lies near the village, with stalactites and stalagmites in a tunnel 834 metres long with a height of 12 m.

The villages of **Ayios Dimitrios** (Thalames), at an altitude of 440 m., and **Trachila** on the coast stand further to the south. There is a fine cave near **Trachila**, with upper and lower chambers, about 100 metres from the beach. A protective wall guarnds of the entrance. Fresh water may be found inside, in basins whose walls are made of stalacites.

The Christeas tower at Ayios Dimitrios.

The fishing village of Ayios Nikolaos, a pretty place in Messinian Mani.

Artemisia stands among the peaks of Mt Taigetos, with abundant streams.

40. Kalamata - Sparta
(60 kms)

The road leaves Kalamata to the north east, and immediately begins to climb.

This is a fine mountain drive, with dense forests, deep ravines and imposing peaks. This is the route taken by Telemachus, son of Odysseus, on his way to Sparta from Pylos to find Menelaus to ask him about the fate of his father.

Halfway along the route, is **Artemissia**, the last village in Messinia (altitude 700 metres), on a beautiful site.

Between here and the Mele Castle is a monastery of St John the Baptist, while at **Ladas**, not far off, is the 14th century 'Pamegiston Taxiarchon' Monastery, with a carved wooden screen and wall paintings.

A minor road north out of Artemisia leads to **Alagonia** and **Nedousa**, of which the former (770 metres) is a popular holiday resort with camp sites. There was an ancient city of the same name nearby, with temples to Artemis and Dionysus.

The hunting is good in the area, and the nearby monasteries of Mardaki (15th century), Sideroporta (16th century) and St Anthony (with fine wall paintings) are worth a visit. There are also ruins of a monastery dedicated to St John the Baptist.

After Artemisia the road continues east into Laconia, towards Sparta.

Map of the Prefecture of Lakonia

LACONIA

Laconia covers the southeastern extremity of the Peloponnese. This is the centre of the culture of the ancient Doric peoples, who first brought iron into the life of ancient Greece.

The terrain is generally mountainous, with a warm, dry climate and a moderate rainfall. The Prefecture has an area of 3,636 square kilometres and a population of 93,000. The area is dominated by the parallel mountain ranges of Parnon and Taigetos, the latter of which is the highest mountain in the Peloponnese at 2,520 metres. The river Eurotas crosses the Prefecture, rising at the Longara springs near the village of Skortsinos. The plain formed by its valley is the most important low-lying part of the Prefecture of Lakonia. In some places, the mountain ranges run right down to the sea, forming a steep coastline of wild, forbidding beauty (as in the Mani). Small gulfs and sheltered bays break up this coastline, creating a variety of landscape of rare grandeur as stark tones are succeeded by gentler ones, all of them with the austerity and power which is the hallmark of the Doric order, born here in Lakonia.

The Doric culture, which in ancient times focused on Sparta and in more modern days found its supreme expression in the customs and habits of the Mani, is a unique phenomenon in Greece, comparable perhaps only to the culture of Corsica. It certainly makes this part of the Peloponnese different from any other.

Life around the feet of Mt Taigetos —which the ancient historian Polybius compared to the Alps— is, of course, quite different to what it was when the Bacchae roamed the area conducting their rituals in honour of Apollo/Bacchus.

185

The Doric invasion and the foundation of the city of Sparta created, in historical times, a city-state which was run on the oligarchic principle. Its laws were formulated by Lycurgus, and their spirit was an unusual kind of equality between free citizens. It was Sparta which, to a large extent, determined the fate of the Peloponnese as a whole. With Athens, it stands supreme in the history of Greece down to the time of Alexander the Great. Sparta was the centre of an important culture whose central aim was its endeavour to inculcate a particular type of morality and mentality. The heritage which it has left us may include no Parthenons, but the ancient Spartans bequeathed one symbol which has come down the centuries undamaged: the bravery of Leonidas and his three hundred warriors, who at Thermopylae gave their lives to impede the advance of those who were invading their native land. The ancient Greeks were well aware of the importance of Sparta; they had a saying which ran, "τό λακωνίζειν ἐστί φιλοσοφεῖν", which means, 'to express oneself as do the Spartans (i.e. *laconically*) is an indication of philosophy'. As Plutarch wrote, "all the Greeks know what is right, but only the Spartans do it properly".

This is confirmed by a story which has come down to us from ancient times:

Once, at the Olympic Games, a venerable old man was passing through the crowd of spectators in search of a seat. Intent on what was going on, everyone ingored his plight; it was only the Spartans who stood up and offered him a place.

The superiority of the Spartan spirit is also demonstrated by their refusal, when they were victorious in the Peloponnesian War, to demolish Athens altogether, as their allies wanted them to.

The Spartans continued to be free-minded and uncompromising people right down to the time of the Romans, when their city went into decline. However, the inner dynamics of history and certain historical conditions brought about the rise, in the 13th century, of another important city in the same area: Mystras, which at one time had a population of 40,000. This fortress-town town was sometimes called the Florence of the East; even into the 16th century, when the rest of Greece was under Turkish rule, Mystras kept Lakonia independent. In later times, it strove to maintain its privileges even under the Turks, the Venetians and the Turks once more.

The tough and unforgiving aspect of their natural surroundings and their long and unceasing fight for independence from the various invaders of their land, has made the Lakonians what they are today. Dark in appearance, with black hair and eyes, they are straightforward people who look life square in the face. Even today, they are specially proud when they can say that they are Maniots —people of the Mani, that is.

In reality, the Mani is only one part of Lakonia, however important it may be, but since Byzantine times it has played the principal role in shaping the identity of the area. The Mani is divided into three parts, Inner, Outer and Lower (see p. 205).

The Inner Mani is the heart of the area; that is where the local customs are still pure and alive. And the traditions of the Mani are descended directly from the austere spirit of ancient Sparta.

The main street of Sparta, with Mt Taigetos in the background.

Sparta

The road from Kalamata begins to descend through thickly wooded gorges, the most famous of which is that known as Megali Langada. We pass **Trypi** (600 m.), where there are abundant streams and a fine view. Nearby is the Kaiadas, the ravine into which the Spartans cast sick or weak children. Then we come to the **Magoulas** crossroads (for Mystras and Ayia Irini and Longaniko), before entering the capital of Laconia.

Sparta (known in Greek as Sparti) has a history which dates back to the Neolithic period, at least 3,000 years before the birth of Christ. The name has a number of possible derivations: the mythical daughter of Evrotas, the mythical Lelege king Sparton or Spar-to, or words connected with the fertility of the sourrounding plain. There were, originally, four settlements: Limnai, Litane, Mesoa and Cynosura, which later became joined together. However, these events are so far distant in the past that only guesses can be made. The Homeric myths and other traditions do help us to see the close links that must have existed between Sparta and the Myceneans and their civilisation. Historians agree that Sparta was a purely Doric city, a result of the new order of things that the Dorians had brought to the Peloponnese. Lycurgus is traditionally credited with the organisation of the militaristic and aristocratic regime of Sparta, although historians now doubt whether there ever was such a person. However this may be, the myths have it that it was Lycurgus who instituted the basic Spartan legislation, divided the area up into equal plots and shared them out between the free citizens, brought in metal currency and enforced military discipline and communal (and spartan!) feeding arrangements.

In Sparta at this time, both public and private life were highly militarised, with barrack life, army food, whippings, unusual marital relations, large numbers of slaves (the Helots), and the exposure of new-born but imperfect children in the gorges of Mt Taïyetos as features of day-to-day existence. The lives of all were in the hands of the powerful and mysterious Ephors from the 8th century on.

The regions around Sparta were the first to feel the force of the city's policy of expansion. It took the Spartans from 743 to 628 to completely subdue neighbouring Messinia, but when they did finally succeed, the conquest was total. In the 7th century there were lyrical poets in Sparta, however — Alcman and Tyrtaeus were outstanding.

The statue of Leonidas, who performed at deed of great heroism at Thermopylae.

Lykurgus, who organised ancient Sparta and gave it laws.

After the 7th century, Sparta was openly attempting to conquer the whole of the Peloponnese, starting off with the Arcadians and Argos. In 572, after the defeat of Pisa, Sparta became unrivalled master of the Sanctuary at Olympia, and began to seek a role in the wider Greek world. Chilon, one of the seven sages of antiquity, famous for the epigrammatic quality of his speech, was an Ephor of note at Sparta in about 556. Thus Sparta come to control three-fifths of the Peloponnese and became, after Athens, the largest power in Greece, and a clash between the two was inevitable. The rivalry first came to a head in 520, when Cleomenes I captured Athens and deposed Hippias, although the Athenians later won their city back.

The Spartans took no part in the first Persian War, but they fought bravely in the second, and Leonidas and his three hundred men wrote one of the brightest pages in history with their sacrifice at Thermopylae. The general period of unrest which followed boiled over into the catastrophic Peloponnesian War, 431-404, which ended with complete victory for Sparta. But only a few years later, when the Greek world discovered that the Spartans were even worse masters than the Athenians had been, the conquests were swallowed up in the Corinthian War. Further wars led to a further weakening of Spartan power, and although Agis and Cleomenes III tried to make radical changes in the social system of the city during the 3rd century BC, their attempts failed. The united army of the Achaean League defeated Sparta at Selasia in 222-221 with the help of the Macedonians, and liberated all the areas which Sparta had conquered over the years. The Roman period was one of steady decline. The final destruction of the city came at the hands of Alaric and his Goths in 396 AD. In the 9th century, Slav attacks forced the populace to hide in the mountains of the Mani. The Byzantines repopulated the town, but it was always under the shadow of nearby Mystras, later being captured by Franks, Venetians and Turks.

The modern town (founded by decree in 1834) is built mainly on the right bank of the river Evrotas, in approximately the same position as the ancient city, whose ruins surround it. Among the most important remains are: a small temple (wrongly identified as 'Leonidas' tomb'), the Agora, a theatre, the temple of Athena Chalkioikos, the temple of Artemis Orthia (where the whipping of young men, to encourage stamina, took place), more recent walls (the first Spartans built no city walls, declaring that their walls were the breasts of their warriors), the acropolis, various Roman and Byzantine buildings, among which is a bridge over the Evrotas, etc.

The Archaeological Museum contains Neolithic pottery, tools and jewellery from the Alepotrypa cave and from Diros, pots, weapons and other objects from Menelaio and Mycenean tombs, classical sculpture and works from the Hellenistic and Roman periods, Geometric and Achaean pottery and friezes, ancient ceramic masks, etc. There is also a Cathedral Museum with post-Byzantine icons and carved crosses.

The garden of Sparta Archaeological Museum, with statuary.

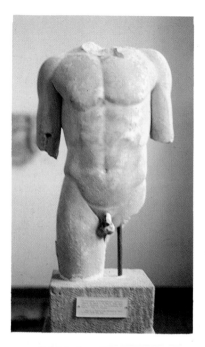

Exhibits from Sparta Museum.

The Byzantine fortified town of Mystras.

Mystras

Mystras is a unique example of a complete Byzantine fortress-town, in ruins and largely overgrown, but none the less interesting for that. It can be approached from Sparta by bus through the modern village of Mystras (camp site) and may be entered either from the top or the bottom. Those who have transport at their disposal may prefer to enter from the top and walk down (as being less tiring) and then catch the bus back up to the top.

After the villages of **Parori** and **Mystras**, there is a tourist pavillon at the **Marmara** place.

The walls which protected the medieval city of **Mystras** may still be seen in quite good repair.

One part of the Cathedral complex is used as a Museum, and preserves pieces of mural, sculptures, pottery, jewellery, metalwork, coins and inscriptions from the last period of Byzantium.

The cathedral church of St Demetrius has a plaque with a double-headed eagle (symbol of Byzantium) recording the crowning of Emperor Constantine.

Of the churches, Ayioi Theodori, the oldest church (1290-1296), a cruciform octagon, with a large dome, had fine wall-paintings which time has nearly destroyed.

The most impressive building is the Palace of the Despots, which was originally the residence of the

MYSTRAS

1. Villehardouin Castle
2. Ayia Sofia
3. Upper Castle Gate
4. Nafplio Gate
5. Palace of the Despots
6. Monemvasia Gate
7. St Nicholas.
8. Pantanassa Convent
9. Perivleptou Convent
10. House of Krevatas
11. Marmara Fountain
12. Cathedral (Museum)
13. Evangelistria
14. Sts Theodore
15. Aphendiko (Our Lady Hodegetria)

Frankish commander of the area. When it became the seat of the Cantacuzene and Palaeologue families, additions were made. The last Byzantine Emperor, Constantine XI, was crowned in the old Cathedral and lived in the Palace (1443-48).

The castle at the top was built (as usual) by the Villehardouins, and the city is full of the ruins of Byzantine churches of great architectural skill, which in their heyday must have been marvels of wall and icon-painting.

The Hodegetria Monastery is a combination of basilica and five-domed cruciform styles with fine paintings and icons. A similar style of church can be found in the Pantanassa Nunnery, which also has a fine view. Folk paintings with scenes of Byzantine life may be bought.

Ayia Sofia was the Palace church. In the castle, the commander's quarters, the walls, a church and other buildings are to be seen. The view is unforgettable: the gorge and peaks of Taïyetos on one side, the river Evrotas and its plain on the other.

Among other interesting buildings is the Perivleptou Monastery, with exceptionally fine wall-paintings.

Generally speaking, Mystras should be visited early in the morning when the heat is less severe. The wild flowers of spring should not be missed either.

Right, the Pantanassa Monastery and below, a wall-painting from its interior.

41. Sparta - Yeraki
(40 kms)

The main Sparta-Tripoli road, which leaves Sparta in a north-easterly direction, divides at 2 kilometres into two smaller roads.

The one leads east, to Chrysafa, and enables the traveller to visit the Ayioi Saranta Monastery, built into the rock. There are interesting icons of the 14th century and a museum with icons, vestments and bulls (late Byzantine).

Chrysafa (250 metres), which probably dates from the 12th century, was named after the wife of an Emperor of Byzantium. There are fine paintings in the Churches of Our Lady 'Chrysafiotissa' (1290) and All Saints (1367). The church of St Demetrius (1641) is also of interest. A monastery of St John the Baptist stands near the village.

Kalloni (Perpeni, to the south east) and **Agrioani** (north east) are interesting mountain villages in the neighbourhood.

The village of **Kallithea** (Zarafona) has a 12th century church with wall-paintings, and there is a well-preserved ancient tower in the vicinity.

The road which forks south from the Sparta-Tripoli road continues parallel to the Evrotas, through **Amfisio, Zagano, Platania** and **Skoura** before entering **Goritsa**. The ancient city of **Therapne** lay between Goritsa and Chrysafa on a ridge known as **Menelaio**.

The city's name came from a daughter of Lelegas, and various find show that it was linked not only with the Myceneans but also with the rest of the Mediterranean and pre-Greek world. According to the myths, the tomb of Menelaus and Helen was at Therapne.

About 40 kilometres south east from Sparta, we come to the historic town of **Yeraki** (320 metres). The site is a very ancient one, probably that of the ancient city of **Geronthae**. The ancient acropolis (6th century) was fortified with a Cyclopean wall (of which ruins can be seen). But finds from the site go back even further, and there is evidence of habitation in the Neolithic and Bronze Ages, about 4000-2500 BC. The inhabitants stood up to the Dorian invasion and kept their independence until around 700 BC. When the Dorians finally took the city, they turned out the former occupants and began a period of reform which turned the area into an important commercial centre, but under the domination of Sparta.

The town escaped from the influence of the Spartans during the Roman period. Pausanias mentions a temple to Apollo on the acropolis, and that there was a temple of Ares in a grove, where an annual ceremony from which women were banned was held. The town kept its commercial position through the first centuries of Christianity. Progress continued through the Frankish period, when Yeraki (as it was by now called) was the seat of one of the twelve Frankish baronies. During Turkish occupation Yeraki was under the protection of the Sultan's harem, and thus enjoyed relative freedom.

During the War of Independence, in which Yeraki played an important part, being burnt down by Ibrahim in August 1825 in revenge, Kolokotronis addressed a call to arms to the Greeks on a hill near the town in September 1825.

The churches of Yeraki are widely known both for their architecture and the beauty of their decoration. The best preserved is of St John Chrysostome (1460), and others worth seeing are: St Sozon (12th century, with a mosaic floor), the Annunciation (with 15th century wall-paintings), St. George (a 3rd century basilica with fine wall-paintings and a rare carved limestone icon stand), the Prophet Elijah, the churches of the Epiphany and the Archangels (a basilica with a cruciform roof, 13th century), and Zoodochos Pighi (1431), a domed basilica with fine wall-paintings, including a superb representation of Christ in Chains. The small museum has a collection consisting mostly of architectural decorative features and gravestones.

Some of the old houses still have their fine wooden yard gates sheltered by domes.

Fine examples of the local weaving tradition have been preserved (rugs, carpets, etc.) showing scenes from everyday life and the myths.

42. Sparta - Tripoli
(60 kms)

The main road to Tripoli (see p. 106) leaves Sparta to the north. On the slopes of Mt Taïyetos, which can be seen from this road, are the masses of olive trees which produce the olive oil for which this region is famous.

A short distance outside Sparta is the village of **Kladas**; it was near here that some of the ancients located the Garden of the Hesperides, where Paris judged a goddesses' beauty contest and awarded the prize to Aphrodite.

At the highest point on the Sparta-Tripoli road the view towards the Taïyetos and Parnon ranges and the small valley of ancient Oenoe and the Evrotas valley is breathtaking.

Just before it enters the Prefecture of Arcadia, at 27 kilometres from Sparta, the road forks; to the left we can reach, in 9 kms, the village of **Karyes** (at 880 metres) and then **Arachova**, or Greater Arachova, which was of some importance in Frankish times. There are very few remains to mark the site of the ancient city of **Carya**, where Artemis and the nymphs were worshipped. In front of an outdoor statue of Artemis a dance said to have been devised by Castor and Pollux was performed by athletic maidens, who were to be the inspiration for the female forms used in ancient times instead of pillars in buildings such as the Erechtheum at Athens and called 'Caryatids' after the name of this place.

43. Sparta - Monemvasia
(96 kms)

The main road continues through Sparta to the south. About 5 kilometres out we pass through **Amykles**, on the site of an ancient city of the same name.

The church of St Kyriaki is built on the sanctuary of Amyclean Apollo and the grave of Hyacinthus, son of Amyclas, where annual celebrations were held.

To the south of Ayia Kyriaki is the village of **Vafeio**, where Mycenean tombs with very significant contents have been found. The most important of these, such as two golden cups with scenes hammer-beaten on them, are now in the Athens Archaeological Museum.

After 8 kilometres there is a turning to the right, leading to **Anoyeia, Paliopanayia** and **Poliana-Doriza**, (830 metres) which is the starting-point for the ascent of Mt Taïyetos. There is a mountain shelter at **Varvara**, 1,600 metres up.

At **Hani Tarapsas** the road forks. The right fork carries on to Yitheio, and we take the left.

This road turns east and soon enters **Krokees**. Here there were famous quarries, which produced Lapis Lacedaemonius, much sought-after for temples, palaces and other public buildings.

After **Skala**, approximately 48 kilometres from Sparta, there is a bridge over the Evrotas, after which a minor road leads north to **Vrontamas**. From the same crossroads a minor road leads south to **Elos**.

We soon come to the turning for **Apidia**, built on the site of ancient **Come**. Ruins exist of an Archaic wall, and there is also a 14th century Byzantine church of the Dormition of the Virgin as well as the ruins of other Byzantine churches.

Just before Molai a road east leads to **Metamorfosis**, where there is a Byzantine church at the 'Kangania' Monastery, set in a beautiful spot among plane trees and cypresses.

The same side road leads on to **Reichia, Achladokambos, Lambokambos, Haraka, Kyparissi, Paralia Yerakas**, and **Limani Yerakas**, the last three of which are on the coast in the extreme north east of Laconia.

The fine town of **Molai** stands on the site of ancient **Leuke**. The nearby ravine, Haradra, has thick vegetation and abundant swift-flowing water, which for centuries was used to turn water-mills.

At **Paliopyrgos**, above the ravine, are ruins of a fortress and walls, as well as a Byzantine church of Sts. Constantine and Helen. The 19th century church of St George has an interesting carved screen.

After **Sykia**, the road forks, the southern part leading through **Velies, Talanta, Elika, Pantanassa** and elsewhere before ending at **Neapoli**, on the coast opposite **Elafoniso**.

The town stands on the site of ancient **Boiai**, always an important port for the Spartans, which reached its zenith in Roman times and had temples to Asclepius, Serapis and Isis.

The harbour of Yerakas.

Today **Neapoli** is a port of some importance and has a daily ferry service to the island of Cythera, a place of geographical importance, much history, wild and barren beauty and numerons monuments.

A minor road leaves Neapoli to the south, crossing the peninsula, and leads to famous Cape Malea ('Kavo Malias'.

The 'beaches' of Elafonissos are covered with shells worn down by the sea.

Kato Kastania lies 17 kilometres to the east of Neapoli. Nearby is the Ayios Andreas cave, which is well worth a visit for its fine displays of stalactites and stalagmites.

After Sykia the main road from Molai continues south east and ends at **Yefira**, next to the singular rock on which stands Monemvasia. Yefira is especially rich in fish, notably mullet and lobster, with which the town once supplied Rome. The area was also famous for its wine, drunk in England as Malmsey.

Monemvasia's name means 'one entrance', and this really is true, as there is only one land approach, now spanned by a narrow bridge. The rock was isolated by an earthquake in 375 AD, which cut it off from the mainland.

The promontory was originally called Minoa, and was a Cretan naval station. Its strong position encouraged the Laconians to use it as a fort against invaders and pirates during the Middle Ages, and it was thus that they saved themselves from the Avars in 558.

Soon after this the Byzantine town seems to have been founded. Churches and palaces were built, and both the Lower and the Upper City were walled, so that the town was known as the 'Gibraltar of the East'.

It was occupied in 1248 by William de Villehardouin, but he was soon forced to give it up to the Byzantines. It then changed hands between the Venetians and the Turks. In 1770, Turkish and Albanian forces took severe reprisals on Monemvasia for

The rock of Monemvasia (= 'single entrance',

participating in the Oreoff rebellion. It finally came into Greek hands, after a three-month siege, in July 1821.

Nowadays, there are very few inhabitants on the rock, which attracts large numbers of foreign tourists every summer. The walk around the ruins of the Upper City should on no account be missed, however, though as with Mystras the early morning and evening are recommended in view of the stiff climb up to the top.

There are a number of fine Byzantine churches, the best being that of 'Elkomenos Christos' (Christ in Chains), built before the 12th century and restored in the 17th, of Byzantine-Ionian style. There are also: Our Lady 'Chrysafitissa', built

passage´).

A section of the medieval town.

Monemvasia, a medieval castle symbolising strength hewn from the rock; high up, the church of Ayia Sofia, guarding the view over infinity.

in the 17th century on the site of an older church, St Paul (18th century), St Stephen of Crete and Our Lady of Crete (early 18th century), St Nicholas (18th century), St Anne, etc. Perhaps the finest of all, however, is Ayia Sophia, built by the Emperor Andronicus II in the 14th century on the edge of a precipitous cliff, on the same pattern as the Dafni Monastery on the outskirts of Athens. Under Our Lady Chrysafitissa is the only spring in Monemvasia, the water of which is said to be efficacious in cases of sterility, especially when sons are desired. The view, especially at sunset, is incredible, covering the sea, the mountains and the town beneath.

There is a small museum in the mosque opposite the Elkomenos church, with a collection of Frankish and Byzantine sculpture.

A little to the north of Yefira are the remains of **Epidaurus Limera**, established by refugees from Epidaurus in Argos. There were temples to Aphrodite, Athena, Zeus and Artemis Limnatis, as well as a wall down to the sea and an acropolis.

A pretty street in Monemvasia; in the background, the belfry of the church of Christ Chained (12th century).

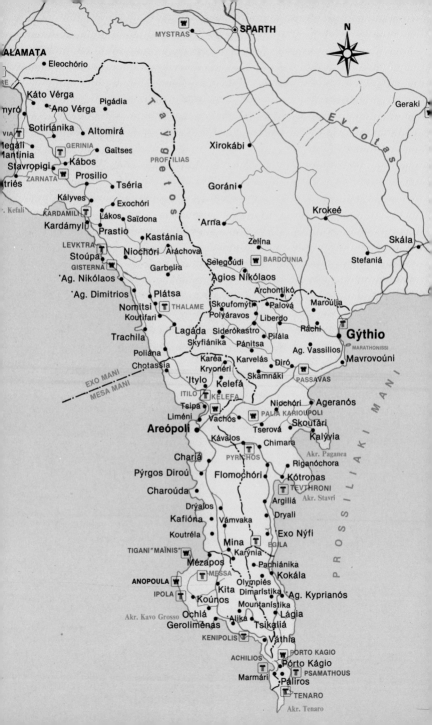

The Mani

This region has customs and habits which remind us that, despite the changes which modern development has brought with it, here in the Mani, in Lakonia, a very closed system of values grew up which focused on the clan, the line of descent, the family — a family which was frequently at odds not only with intruders from outside but also with other Maniot families. These disputes between families could not always be solved by peaceful means. The type of life these people led in these closed systems left its traces on their customs and practices.

It is no coincidence that here, even more than in the rest of Greece, great importance was attached to the birth of male children. And when marriages were in the offing, what was important to the Maniots was the number of new 'rifles' that the union would bring. Brides with numerous brothers were much sought-after.

There were different customs, too, for when the bride arrived at her new home; whereas in the rest of Greece the bride is supposed to throw confetti or be spoon-fed with honey, in the Mani she is supposed to throw coins — to demonstrate her intention to have lots of boy children.

The women of the Mani led lives which were just as hard as those of the men. They did their fair share of the work in the fields and, of course, had the housework on top of that. Women had a special role, too: that of singing the dirges which made the Mani famous throughout Greece for their power and beauty. These are songs of death, songs of mourning for those who are leaving this transient world. And it is the women, who bring life into the

A map of the Mani, showing the local divisions, the positions of the ancient cities and the sites of Byzantine and more modern castles.

world, who close the circle by singing its unexpected end. The dirge-singers are reminiscent of nothing so much as the chorus in the ancient tragedy. In the dirges of the Mani, love of life is expressed in the form of pain and passion, and sometimes fear of death can be transformed into contempt and fearlessness. The women sing these dirges with their long hair let down; most of the time the music and the words are improvised as the singers are inspired, spontaneaously, by the memory of the tradition which they bear within them.

The Mani is also famous for its unusual architecture: this takes the form of tower-houses, which sometimes are as much as four storeys in height. These towers, which were sometimes self-contained houses and were sometimes built on to existing houses, were a type of fortress intended to protect the family from its neighbours and other enemies. All the villages with towers are now under protection orders, and many of them have been converted into excellent private hotels, where visitors can enjoy modern comforts in an environment remiscent of an age when life was much more difficult.

The Maniots of the present no longer spend their time warring with pirates, corsairs, Turks, Venetians and each other. They tend their olive trees, which produce excellent fruit, their citrus trees, their tiny wheat-fields, their cotton crops and their pigs, which produce particularly tasty meat used in the making of 'synklina': salt pork sausage. In the coastal villages, fishing is an important occupation. Nowadays, the Maniots look after the tourist trade as well, an area of the economy which is developing thanks to the fact that along with its natural beauties —which include a number of unique phenomena, such as the Diros Caves— Lakonia can offer its visitors a wealth of history and unusual customs.

Yitheio

The Tzanetakis tower on Kranai.

After covering 46 kilometres south from Sparta, we enter the capital of the Mani, **Yitheio,** supposedly built by Heracles and Apollo.

It was a Spartan naval station, and frequently attacked by Athenian forces. Indeed, the Athenian admiral Tolmides destroyed it in 455. The town was rebuilt later, and flourished under the Romans, only to disappear again and resurface only in 1687, as a small port. In 1770 it was known as Marathonisi, and was a major centre of the Greek Revolution. It took its ancient name again when liberated in 1821.

The coastal road near Gytheio.

The little island of **Kranai** —or **Marathonisi**— was a port of call for the Phoenicians when fishing for purple-dye. The Phoenicians went so far as to build a temple to Aphrodite on the island, which is also traditionally the place where Paris and Helen spent their first night when fleeing from Sparta.

Today a restored medieval castle can be seen there. Of the ancient city, there are remains of the acropolis, the theatre (cultural events in the summer) and some Roman buildings and Emperor's palaces.

South of Yitheio is Mavrovouni, with a fine sandy beach, afterwards the road leads west to Areopoli.

Areopoli is the centre of the Mani.

It stands at an altitude of 250 metres, and has cobbled streets, Maniot towers, stone-built houses and old churches. The entire town is under a preservation order. There is an interesting 18th church (of the Archangels). The stone in which the local people rested the flag pole during the Revolution can also be seen.

A view of Areopoli; the tower of the church of the Archangels can be discerned.

Limeni Bay, with Neo Itilio by the sea (above), and (below), Palaio Itilo further inland among its cypress trees.

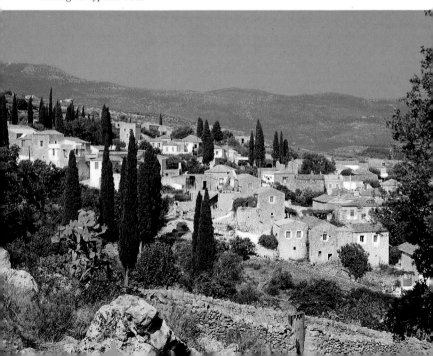

To the north of Aeropoli, the road runs down to the coast of the Messinian Gulf and to **Limeni,** the harbour of Aeropoli. This is an attractive traditional village, with the restored tower of War of Independence hero Petrobey Mavromichalis, which is used as a museum. Still further north we come to Itylo and into Messinia.

Itylo is a pretty and verdant village, quite a surprise after the aridity of the Mani. There are traditional two-storeyed tower houses but the architecture is not pure Maniot. The doors and windows are small, but painted bright blue, thus seltting up a vivid contrast with the red tiles of the roofs. On a quiet bay is **Neo Itylo**, the port for the area.

On a hill above Neo Itylo, in an area with a typical craggy Mani landscape, are the remains of the medieval castle of Kelephas.

To the south of Areopoli, after **Dryalia**, the road forks. The eastern fork leads to **Pyrichos** (400 metres) and **Loukadika** before ending at Kotronas. On its peaceful bay, this is the largest coastal village of the eastern Mani.

Near Kotronas was the ancient city of **Teu hrone**, with its spring, the only one in the region. A minor road from Kotronas leads to the Monastery of the Saviour.

Limeni, a pretty village from which the Mavromichalis family originated.

Flomochori.

Further south of Kotronas the minor road follows the steep western coast of the Gulf of Laconia. The villages in this area are **Flomochori, Agrilia, Halikia, Korakianika, Kokala, Dimaristika, Ayios Kyprianos, Lagia, Pyrgaros, Akroyali, Koroyanniatika, Kenourio Chorio, Achilleio** and **Marmari**.

The most southerly village in the Peloponnese, **Mianes**, stands on the promontory which ends in Cape Matapan.

After the Dryalia crossroads, the road from Areopoli continues south, along the much-indented coastline of the Gulf of Messinia.

The strange Maniot towers can be seen from time to time rearing themselves above the surrounding countryside and their ruins can be found in most of the villages. These multi-storey buildings, which give the impression of being some kind of fortification, were actually built to be lived in, but the element of fortification was added by the local builders because in times past the whole extended family would frequently be besieged inside in the course of local blood feuds or attacks by foreign enemies.

The road passes the bay of Diros, where the Maniot womens heroically beat off the forces of Ibrahim in 1826. Today it is better known internationally for its caves, which may be reached from the village of **Pyrgi Dirou**, which stands on the coast at a height of 200 metres.

THE GLYFADA CAVE DIROS

RED CHAMBER

DRAGON'S LAIR

WHITE CHAMBERS

HANGING BEDS OF THE WATER-SPRITES

PINK CHAMBER

GREAT OCEAN

CATHEDRAL

GREAT LAKE

DOCKS

MANMADE ENTRANCE

NATURAL ENTRANCE

The **Glyfada** cave is one of the world's most beautiful. There is a whole maze of underground passages and chambers, and the visitor may take a trip of some 2 kms in a small boat through these channels. The stalactites and stalagmites are extremely memorable. The underground river Vlychada flows through this underworld.

Nine large chambers, divided by massive columns of stalagmites and narrow passageways and three small lakes with white bottoms cover an imposing area of 9,000 square metres. Speleologists discovered in the Glyfada cave in 1983 the crystallised skeleton of large carnivorous animal, probably a panther. Many areas of the cave are as yet unexplored and it is likely that there will be other interesting finds here in the future.

The **Alepotripa** cave, some 200 metres to the east, consists of three underground lakes. One of these is 25 metres by 40 metres and archaeological finds from its depths have shown that it was used as a place of worship in ancient times. The caves takes its name ('foxhole') from its chance finding in 1958, when a fox which was being pursued sought refuge in it.

Another 300 metres to the West is the **Katafygi** cave, used as a shelter during the Revolution. It has a total length of 450 metres, with many chambers and galleries, and small lakes with stalactites and stalagmites. Traces of a very ancient footprint have been found here.

Another attractive, smaller, cave is that which goes by its medieval name of **Tsita Vekia** (Città Vecchia) on the eastern side of the Bay of Diros. Below the cave are beaches with provision for visitors.

Other interesting caves are to be found further south, notably the Vouyorgi cave, which lies between **Frangoulias** and **Dryalos**. It has stalactites and stalagmites and a chamber measuring 16 × 25 metres.

Continuing south, we come to the village of **Mezapo**, built on the site of the harbour of the ancient city of **Messa**.

In wild, rocky country near **Mina** is the **Alatsospilo** cave, which has a wide passage leading on to a platform above the sheer cliff.

Further along are the villages of **Kitta** and **Nomia**.

The underground river of Glyfada at Diros, described as one of the world's most beautiful cave lakes.

Vatheia or Polypyrgos, a traditional Maniot village; below, Yerolimenas from the sea.

The Mani ends at Cape Tenaron, the mythical entrance to Underworld.

The road leads to **Yerolimenas**, a pretty village built under a cliff on the site of the ancient **Hippola**.

A minor road leaves Yerolimenas in a south easterly direction and leads to the villages of **Alika** and **Vatheia**.

The Maniot towers at Vatheia are one of the most remarkable examples of this particular type of folk architecture. The towers, clustered around the hilltop, gaze proudly out to sea. They have two or three storeys and are constructed of grey stone, with white marble being used only on the corners. The windows are tiny and over the doors are holes for pouring boiling oil over unwelcome visitors. Taken together, these towens make up an impregnable castle.

Today many of the have been restored and are in use as tourist accommodation.

The southern extremity of the Mani is best approached by caïque from Yerolimenas. Rounding the headland by boat is an unforgettable experience. The caïque puts in at Marmari or Porto Marinari.

A short distance away is the small peninsula which ends in Cape Matapan (Tainaro).

This was the site of the ancient city of Taenaron, built by an eponymous son of Zeus. There was a famous sanctuary of Poseidon and the ancients believed that what are now called the Ayii Asomati caves on the cape were one of the entrances to Hades.

MAP OF ARCHAEOLOGICAL SITES AND CAVES

PATRA

KORINTHOS

Korinthos

MYKINES

EPIDAVROS

PYRGOS

OLYMPIA

TIRYNTHA

NAFPLIO

TRIPOLI

VASSES

ITHOMI

SPARTI

NESTORA PALACE

KALAMATA

DYROU

KYTHIRA

🏛 Archaeological Sites

1. Iréo
2. Elíki
3. Sykión
4. Lécheo
5. ´Isthmia
6. Ilis
7. Stýmfalos
8. Flioús
9. Neméa
10. Orchomenós
11. Assini
12. Trizýna
13. Skilountia
14. Mantinia
15. Tegéa
16. Górtyna
17. Megalópolis
18. Lépreon
19. Lykóssoura
20. Sellassìa
21. Spárti
22. Amýkles
23. Faré
24. Pýlos
25. Epìdavros Lymirá

🏛 Caves

1. Trikálon
2. Néstoros

MAP OF PRINCIPAL CASTLES AND MONASTERIES

PATRA
MEGA SPILEO
AGIAS LAVRAS
KORINTHOS
AKROKORINTHOS
PYRGOS
NAFPLIO
NAFPLIO
TRIPOLI
VOULKANOU
SPARTI
KALAMATA
MYSTRAS
GERAKI
METHONI
MONEMVASSIA
KYTHIRA

♜ Castles

1. Río
2. Pátra
3. Kounoupelioú
4. Glarétzas
5. Chlemoútsi
6. Pontikoú
7. ´Argous
8. Moúchli
9. Karítena
10. Niklí
11. ´Astros
12. Oriá
13. Kyparissía
14. Androúsi
15. Kalamón
16. Navarínou
17. Koróni
18. Zarnatás
19. Passavá
20. Kelefá
21. Portokalíou

🏛 Monasteries

1. Potápiou
2. Faneroménis
3. Feneoú
4. Taxiarchón
5. Vlachernón
6. Kremastís
7. Kernítsis
8. Filossófou
9. Malévis
10. Élónis
11. Pantánassa
12. Dimióvis

219

The Peloponnese has an area of 21,379 square kilometres. The total population is 1,012,528 (1981 census), the majority of whom are employed in farming and stock-breeding and, more recently, in tourism.

Administratively, the Peloponnese is divided into seven Prefectures: Corinthia (area 2,290 sq. km., population 123,000) with Corinth as its capital, the Argolid (area 2,154 sq. km., population 93,000), with Nafplio as its capital, Arkadia (area 4,418 sq. km., population 108,000), with Tripoli as its capital, Achaia (area 3,271 sq. km., population 275,000), with Patra as its capital (and also as the capital of the whole Peloponnese, with a population of 150,000), Ileia (area 2,617 sq. km., population 160,000), with Pyrgos as its capital, Messinia (area 2,990 sq. km., population 159,000), with Kalamata as its capital, and Lakonia (area 3,636 sq. km., population 93,000), with Sparta as its capital.

	Athina	Korinthos	Patra	Pyrgos	Tripoli	Nafplio	Sparti	Kalamata
ATHINA	—	84	217	315	193	145	254	283
KORINTHOS	84	—	132	231	109	61	169	199
PATRA	217	132	—	98	176	194	302	267
EGIO	176	92	41	139	201	153	261	291
RIO	211	127	7	105	236	188	296	274
PYRGOS	315	231	98	—	151	223	211	169
KYLLINI	290	205	68	38	190	260	250	160
OLYMPIA	234	240	113	20	130	202	193	133
TRIPOLI	193	109	176	151	—	72	60	90
MEGALOPOLI	228	144	211	109	35	107	95	60
NAFPLIO	145	61	194	223	72	—	132	162
ARGOS	133	49	182	211	60	12	120	150
EPIDAVROS	153/177	68/90	201	253	102	30	162	192
SPARTI	254	169	302	211	60	132	—	60
MYSTRAS	259	174	307	216	65	137	5	65
GYTHIO	299	215	348	257	106	178	46	108
MONEMVASSIA	350	265	398	307	156	225	97	154
NEAPOLI	386	303	436	346	195	263	135	195
KALAMATA	283	199	267	169	90	162	60	—
PYLOS	324	240	222	124	131	203	111	51
METHONI	384	261	230	137	152	224	122	62
KYPARISSIA	291	207	154	57	98	171	128	68

CLIMATOLOGICAL PARTICULARS

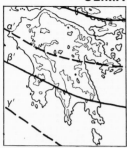

RAINFALL

Average annual air temperature distribution in the Peloponnese:
a)18.5° line
b)19° line
g)19.5° line

400 MM
400 - 600
600 - 800
800 - 1000
1000

Prevailing winds in the Peloponnese

AVERAGE ANNUAL NUMBER OF DAYS OF

	sunshine	cloud	rain	snow	hail	storms	frost
Patra	152	61	98	0.4	3.4	22.0	4.1
Korinth	134	53	62	0.4	0.2	8.3	1.0
Pyrgos	135	49	79	0.4	4.6	10.7	5.1
Nafplio	125	52	73	1.0	0.5	10.5	4.3
Tripoli	115	68	109	7.6	2.2	16.6	38.1
Sparta	130	51	85	2.0	1.7	13.3	6.5
Kalamata	136	62	100	0.1	2.0	16.3	1.1
Methoni	129	60	112	0.3	5.9	34.5	1.1

AVERAGE AIR TEMPERATURE °C

	Jan.	Apr.	July	Okt.	Year
Patra	9.9	15.9	26.7	19.0	17.9
Korinth	10.0	15.8	27.8	19.2	18.3
Pyrgos	10.5	15.8	26.9	19.6	18.2
Nafplio	10.1	15.9	27.7	19.6	18.4
Tripoli	5.2	12.2	24.6	15.1	14.3
Sparta	9.0	15.5	27.2	19.0	17.7
Kalamata	11.2	16.3	27.1	20.2	18.6
Methoni	11.6	16.0	25.4	20.2	18.4

AV. RETATIVE HUDIMITY (%)

	Jan.	Apr.	July	Okt.	Year
Patra	73	69	60	70	68
Korinth	75	68	59	70	68
Pyrgos	78	75	69	76	75
Nafplio	76	68	55	70	67
Tripoli	79	63	46	69	65
Sparta	76	65	49	69	65
Kalamata	73	69	69	71	68
Methoni	74	74	74	73	74

AVERAGE RAINFALL (mm)

	Jan.	Apr.	July	Okt.	Year
Patra	107.8	49.3	2.8	87.0	725
Korinth	63.7	29.8	5.5	60.0	437
Pyrgos	125.2	45.8	1.7	101.5	826
Nafplio	71.8	24.3	4.5	62.5	502
Tripoli	124.5	56.5	18.3	80.8	857
Sparta	120.6	36.4	10.3	81.8	817
Kalamata	141.3	46.1	3.2	91.7	837
Methoni	137.4	30.0	0.5	101.9	767

PREVAILING WINDS

Patra	SW	SW	SW	SW
Korinth	S	NW	NW	S
PYrgos	NW	NW	NW	NW
Nafplio	N	S	S	N
Tripoli	N	SW	N	N
Sparta	N	N	N	N
Kalamata	N	S	S	S
Methoni	N	W	NW	NW

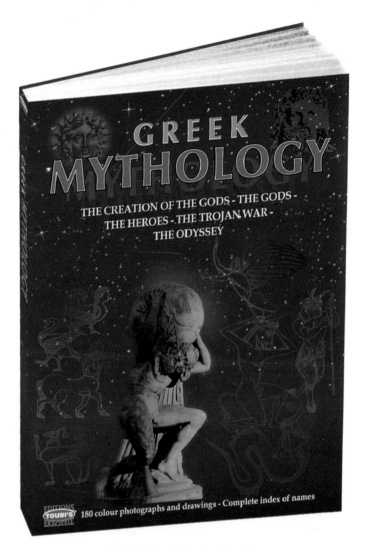

GREEK MYTHOLOGY

This special edition has been designed to present the main Greek myths. A work of considerable scope, written in a simple and expressive language, it is accompanied by 180 photographs and excerpts from ancient Greek literature. Pages: 176, format: 17 × 24 cm

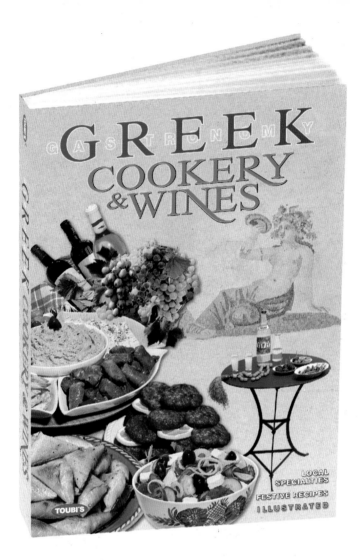

GREEK COOKERY & Wines

$\mathscr{A}$ luxury edition which takes us into the magical world of Greek and Cypriot cuisine with traditional recipes, local specialities, pastries, wines and other beverages, from all the areas of Greece and Cyprus, each recipe with the estimated number of calories. 170 colour photographs, pages: 192, format: 17 × 24

Traveller's map and guide to
the Peloponnese

scale: 1: 485,000

**This detailed map
of the Peloponnese
takes the visitor
around the area
step by step,
it includes diagrams
of the archaeological sites,
useful information and
a brief background text.**

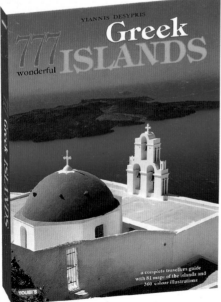

777 *Greek ISLANDS*

*M*any years in preparation,
now completed in 1994.
A unique edition which
treats 777 beautiful
Greek Islands from the
9,500 islands and rocky
outcroppings of the Greek
Archipelago.

*360 colour illustrations,
81 maps of the islands,
format: 17 × 24,
pages: 272*